Radical
Landscapes

Reinventing Outdoor Space

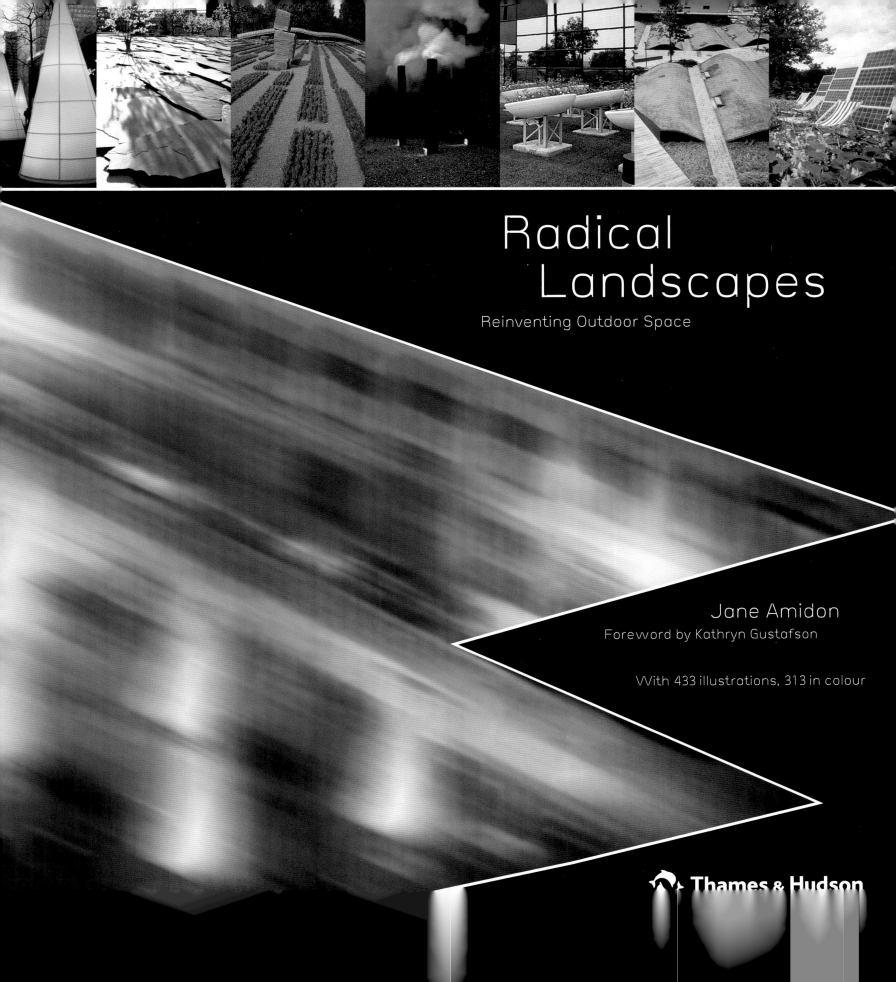

Radical
Landscapes

Reinventing Outdoor Space

Jane Amidon

Foreword by Kathryn Gustafson

With 433 illustrations, 313 in colour

Thames & Hudson

The Task of Translation
by Kathryn Gustafson

As landscape architects and arbiters of cultural expression, we have the capacity to translate. Environmental concerns, clients' programmes and users' needs are raw materials to be measured and patterned and prepared to fit holistically on the land and within its systems. There is an inherent responsibility that accompanies this task: our work has weight and consequences – ecologically, historically, socially – that are dangerous to ignore. One mind, one design instinct, can only benefit from exposure to mixed disciplines – architecture fused with land, art with science, theatre with history and so forth. Collaboration and experimentation bring about complexity and increased comprehension that can broaden an idea's appeal.

The wider our horizon of creation, the more diverse our landscapes become, and the higher the tolerance the public develops to live, work and see things differently. Today we interpret use of public space in a new way and are able to focus on places that had no value twenty years ago. This will continue as we explore how to repair and reuse damaged lands in our industrialized society. In this evolution, a bold intellectual stance and rich emotional palette are essential to creating landscapes that carry a sense of function, time and place.

The projects shown in this book consider various aspects of contemporary place-making. Some offer new paradigms for built landscapes that play a vital role as infrastructure in our cities and in our personal environments. Others, specifically the garden festival installations, expand the edges of experimentation and introduce landscape design to a greater audience but often disregard critical issues that are intrinsic to the practice. Our cultural appetite certainly encompasses both, so let us consume with awareness.

First published in the United Kingdom in 2001 by Thames & Hudson Ltd, 181A High Holborn, London WC1V 7QX
www.thamesandhudson.com

© 2001 Jane Amidon
First paperback edition 2003

British Library Cataloguing-in-Publication Data
A catalogue record for this book is available from the British Library

ISBN 0-500-28427-X

Printed and bound in Hong Kong by Toppan Printing Co.

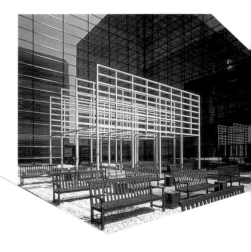

p. 1: Kuala Lumpur International Airport + Eco-Media City, Malaysia (photo by Tomio Ohashi); pp. 2–3: Glowing Topiary Garden, New York, US (photo by Ken Smith); p. 3 from left Glowing Topiary Garden, New York, US (photo by Ken Smith); Interpolis Garden, Tilburg, The Netherlands (photo by Jeroen Musch); Garden for VSB, Utrecht, The Netherlands (photo by Jannes Linders); Après la Grande Tempête – Trois Cheminées de Desmarest, Desmarest, France (photo by David Jones); Hughes Communications Headquarters, Long Beach, California, US (photo by Derek Rath); Yokohama Portside Park, Yokohama, Japan (photo by Studio on Site); Power Plants, Festival International des Jardins, Chaumont-sur-Loire, France (photo by Peter Walker and Partners Landscape Architecture).

Introduction

The dignity of the artist lies in his duty of keeping awake the sense of wonder in the world. In this long vigil he often has to vary his methods of stimulation; but in this long vigil he is also himself striving against a continual tendency to sleep. **G.K. Chesterton**[1]

A Provocative Push

It is human nature to search out the new, the exciting, the source of energy that will release us from bonds of the ordinary, the expected, the known. At the same time, we seek beauty and balance within ourselves and in relation to the world around us. The expression of these objectives continually evolves, and at their intersection, the radical emerges. The radical emerges in all disciplines – art, design, music, literature, theory – it is the provocative push that moves us forward. Unlike the avant-garde movement, which can be said to exist only in opposition and consciously rejects the traditions of its genre[2], the radical impulse is cultivated within existing methods and is an outgrowth of today's trends into tomorrow's realities.

If you open a recently published dictionary, you will note that 'radical' is found below 'radiation sickness' and above 'radicchio'. What more perfect book ends could we ask for to provide societal reference points for works conceived, constructed and presented in reaction to contemporary cultural forces – the one a mid-twentieth-century phantom, the second a culinary icon of fin-de-siècle faddism. Herein is found a critical question to keep in mind as the pages of the book are turned: what are the underlying currents, tectonic forces and ambient factors that generate change in the design of landscape?

Without the capacity for radical thought, evolution would not occur. While some elements of our society value tradition over exploration, the design of the spaces in which we live constantly changes in response to new technologies and cultural shifts. A juror at the 1999 Progressive Architecture Awards for visionary design pointed out that winning entries had several key components: 'future, fantasy, and optimism'. A year later, another juror stated simply that he looked for investigations 'that [didn't] necessarily reaffirm the status quo'[3]. The 'Innovative Houses' show at the Museum of Modern Art in New York proposed that contemporary residential design blurs the distinction between interior/exterior space with an attitude that is 'Hollywood and delirious'.

The suitability of landscape as a venue for experimentation is evidenced by a surge in non-traditional design of public places and semi-private spaces, such as Makoto Sei Watanabe's Village Terrace in Japan (p. 104), Ken Smith's Jardins Mutants scheme (p. 112), or Cheryl Barton's work at the Thoreau Center in San Francisco (p. 170). The growing popularity of garden festivals also points to a new understanding of the garden as a vehicle of contemporary investigation. Annual shows, such as the Festival International des Jardins at Chaumont-sur-Loire in France, the new Festival International des Jardins de Métis at Reford Gardens in Quebec and the Festival of Temporary Gardens in Berlin show signs that garden landscapes are readily visualized not as spatial entities but as malleable media of cultural commentary. As our landscapes progress through various stylistic phases, there remains a perennial tension between contrasting paradigms: outdoor space as an inhabitable volume versus sites crafted as articulated surfaces.

The rise in the number of specifically investigative (non-commercial) garden and landscape shows is notable. Similarly, with increasing frequency, green infrastructure is viewed as a crucial binding fabric in such masterplans of massively scaled, event-oriented landscapes as the Sydney 2000 Olympics (p. 150), with much of its design the result of ecological site research, and the Hanover Expo 2000, which offers a digitally explored and rendered vision of land use. Clearly, they both strive to present radical and educational messages about the intersection of our built and natural environments.

Radical Traces

The role of garden shows and expositions in the dissemination of radical design ideas is by no means new. Landscape historians often cite the 1925 International Exposition of Modern Decorative and Industrial Arts in Paris as a moment when the door opened to modernism in landscape architecture. There, Robert Mallet-Stevens created a garden out of concrete and grass: a four-square of reinforced concrete trees set on two raised beds. It shocked some sensibilities of the day – several critics panned the installation as a travesty to garden science – but ignited others. A second exhibitor, Gabriel Guevrekian, won a Grand Prix with a tiny scheme entitled 'Garden of Water and Light', a mirrored, triangular tableau that was a translation of a two-dimensional graphic rendering. Guevrekian's trend-setting masterpiece, 'a hyphen between architecture and nature – linking the two elements while dividing them'[4], and Mallet-Stevens's use of new technologies and materials, led landscape architects, architects and artists of the day down new paths.

Abstraction in the landscape, unacceptable under the long reign of beaux-arts methodologies, began to trickle in from mainstream culture during the interwar period. Exploratory studies of space and composition on the land, conducted mainly in private settings by such forward-looking designers as the Vera brothers in the 1930s, applied ideas of deconstruction, deanimation, montage and reduction to the garden realm. While seminal tenets of the International Style accepted landscape's status as the untouched Virgilian 'other', suppliant to – or ignored by – architecture's rational stance, radical landscape architects endeavoured to find clients and colleagues open to investigating modern constructs on the land.

The efforts of these visionaries become a powerful force in Western landscape architecture from the 1940s. American landscape architect Fletcher Steele had visited the 1925 Expo in Paris and returned home with a suitcase full of new ideas to share with his stateside colleagues. One important concept was the notion of the architectural garden, which in tune with emerging strains of modernism was to guide the hand and shape the land for decades to come. Steele's willingness to step outside the bounds of tradition served as inspiration for such young designers of his day as Thomas Church, and later, Garrett Eckbo, James Rose and Dan Kiley. Working primarily on the West Coast, Church established a fluid California style that was soon imitated. The work of Eckbo, Rose and Kiley in the United States proclaimed loudly that post-World-War-II landscapes had an agenda and a potential far greater than the prevailing, predictable design tradition. Their push into new territory was fostered by the teachings of, among others, architects Walter Gropius and Ludwig Mies van der Rohe and English landscape architect Christopher Tunnard. In his publication <u>Gardens in the Modern Landscape</u>, Tunnard encouraged garden designers to shake off 'the academic yoke of styles' to be 'free to interpret the message of one's work of art in a new and more forceful manner'[5].

It was not until the 1950s that the well-worn icon of modernism – the grid – became prevalent in garden design. Much of the built work of the time exhibited the hegemony of the grid as a structural and ordering device, as well as representing an intellectual stance. There was also a growing interest in garden design of the Orient, particularly the idea of harmonizing architecture and environment and the precise, modular manipulation of space. This meshed with principles of the Modern Movement to produce such works as the Miller House garden by Dan Kiley in 1955. Although Kiley's use of classic elements to achieve a contemporary sense of spatial structure seemed radical at the time, it is now a mainstay of landscape design. Meanwhile, in South America, landscape architect Roberto Burle Marx was employing a painterly technique to achieve striking articulations of form and flowing colour.

Environmental artists stepped to the radical forefront of art in the late 1960s. It was clear at the time that their massively scaled works moved art out of the grasp of galleries, but it is only in retrospect that it was also seen as a change that forever blurred the lines between art, environment and land design. Governing elements of the natural world – weather, daily cycles, topography, geology, water bodies, the horizon line – became simultaneously the media and the setting in which to portray the human/nature/art dialectic. Is there a more spectacular sculpture garden than Walter de Maria's Lightning Field (New Mexico,1977)?

A new breed of landscape architect was breaking radical ground in the 1970s with forays into minimalist art. In his essay 'Minimalist Gardens Without Walls', Peter Walker proposed to eliminate the framing of gardens within established limits. To do so, he explained, the design must contain at least three ideas that 'command dynamic presence in the landscape: 1) gesture, 2) hardening and flattening of the surface, and 3) seriality'[6]. By the 1980s and into the 1990s, the voice of environmental and minimalist art rang clearly through the ranks of progressive landscape architects. Yet these attitudes were mixed with a re-emerging interest in landscape as a vessel of narration and metaphor. Young firms spoke in a process-based language that focused on site morphology and indicated a new relationship with the industrial legacy. Such designers as Peter Latz in Germany approached the design of outdoor place as an act of interpretation. Latz described the potential of contemporary, cutting-edge landscape architecture as 'the realization of abstract ideas [about] nature, ecology and society'[7]. Importantly, and indicative of many of today's intriguing projects, he points out that 'ecology as art is made visible in landscape architecture by being incorporated into new interpretations of spatial patterns'[8] but that 'the invention of information systems or layers that overlap with existing elements ... must precede any thoughts on appearance or expression.'[9]

Many of the 'radical' trends of the past decades have steadily leached into the mainstream. Often innovators have been labelled seditious, their works not truly of the landscape or garden genre. Once a trailblazer defines legitimate grounds, however, the herald of originality is paid the sincerest form of flattery: imitation.

1 Chesterton, Gilbert Keith. 'On Maltreating Words'. Generally Speaking.
2 Meyer, Elizabeth. 'The Public Park as Avant-Garde (Landscape) Architecture'. Landscape Journal.
3 Barreneche, Raul. 'The Spirit of the New'. Architecture magazine website (April 2000).
4 Imbert, Dorothée. The Modernist Garden in France (New Haven: Yale University Press, 1993).
5 Tunnard, Christopher. Gardens in the Modern Landscape (London: The Architectural Press, 1938): 80.
6 Walker, Peter and Cathy Deino Blake. 'Minimalist Gardens Without Walls'. The Meaning of Gardens. Mark Francis and Randy Hester, eds. (Cambridge: MIT Press): 120–29.
7 Latz, Peter. 'The Idea of Making Time Visible'. Topos (vol. 33, Munich: Callwey-München, December 2000): 95.
8 Ibid: 99.
9 Ibid: 95.
10 Landscape Journal. Special Issue (University of Wisconsin Press, 1998).
11 Cosgrove, Denis. 'The Landscape Idea and the Modern World'. Social Formation and Symbolic Landscape (London: Croom Helm, 1984).

Today

Today we see contemporary themes that may or may not take hold. From broad visions of eco-revelatory design[10] – the marriage of economic and ecological revitalization in the creation of public spaces and regional infrastructure – to the meting out of new standards for the stewardship of cultural landscapes, the radical impulse is oriented toward connecting to a larger context. In the United States, the National Park Service has formed a Cultural Landscape Foundation that may prove, over time, to be instrumental in the identification, evaluation and reinterpretation of significant sites. An evolving awareness exists, a leitmotif that has long been present in the design of the land but that is now coming to the fore: crafted landscape can play an infra-societal – even didactic – role, particularly in urban settings.

More narrowly focused trends are also recognizable, for example, a desire to reveal site-specific micro-conditions, to manipulate topography, to incorporate urban and industrial archaeology, to subvert structural clarity, to emphasize sustainable constructs and materials and to digitally explore hypothetical landscapes. There is an increasing tendency to use plant communities as biological and cultural agents of change on the land; no longer mute form in a spatial or graphic composition, plant species are selected as much for their ability to alter aspects of the existing environment – be it contaminated soils, degraded water systems, eroding shorelines, polluted air, or levels of solar radiation – as for their visual and structural characteristics. Although much of the growing hyper-awareness of our human role in the success or failure of a healthy earth will be relegated to merely symbolic treatment, there is potential to fuse ecological, educational, aesthetic and spiritual mandates into a unified model for designed landscapes.

Dialogue and Diversity

The projects presented here play with traditional assumptions about place, use and meaning in the landscape. In general, this body of work is consistent in its valuing of content and effect over strictly formal concerns. The concepts of 'landscape' and 'garden' are brought forth in a multitude of scales and qualities. Many of the projects are working biological, social or aesthetic models: from storm-water management to reconnection of the pedestrian to the urban network, from a play on the infiltration of technology into our daily environment to moulding contours that catch sunlight and cast shadow, there is a revelation of idiosyncratic details that instill meaning over time.

It seems that designers who view the landscape and the garden as a scene for unconventional exploration are just as likely to be artists, architects or urbanists as landscape architects. Each has a remarkably varied instinct for site disposition and design expression, yet they share an urge to link site conditions to ecological and cultural contexts by unusual programme interpretation, use of materials and formal composition. If one looks closely, common themes emerge from the diversity.

Place-making is a social process, the 'consequence of a collective human transformation of nature'[11]. The reader is invited to proceed with eyes open to the visual detail of each project and with mind open to the dialogue between site and context, between process and permanence, between sensation and memory. It is this exchange that sets the works and their designers apart, a knitting of past to future with the present of the landscape.

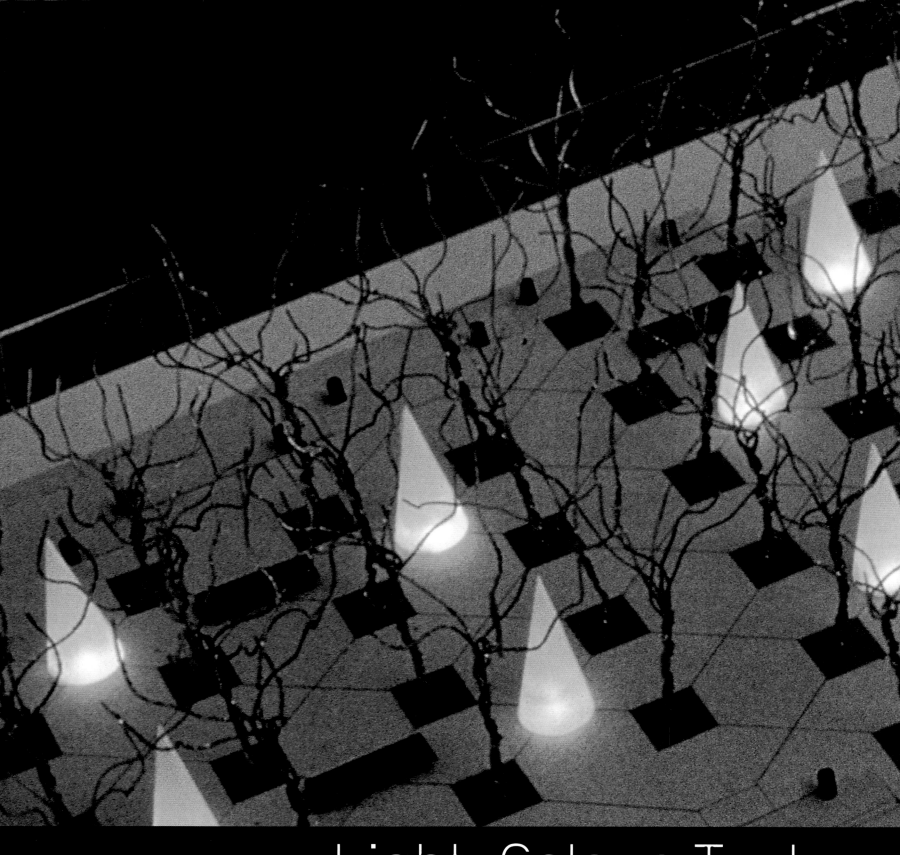

Light, Colour, Texture

Light, colour and texture are tools used to bring forth the solidity of form and shape, yet simultaneously they are evanescent qualities that reveal the innate transitions to which all landscapes are subject.

Architecture is the masterly, correct and magnificent play of masses brought together in light. Our eyes are made to see forms in light; light and shade reveal these forms.
Le Corbusier[1]

There is nothing radical in the revolutionary sense about the use of light, colour and texture in landscape and garden design. In a botanical lexicon, the term 'radical' refers to 'coming from the root'[2], and it is in this context that light, colour and texture are important radical and emotive powers. These elements, perhaps more than any other aspect of a design, can often expose, in the words of garden historian and writer John Dixon Hunt, the fundamental melding of 'site, sight, and insight'[3].

A site that communicates in the languages of light, colour and texture brings the human impulse closer to the natural context, whether the designer chooses to capture ambient effects or to introduce new terms. What stimulates the eye, the mind and the imagination is sensory information, often gathered subliminally as the conscious brain confronts the complexities of form, placement and dimension in its attempt to comprehend functional parameters. Instinctual reactions are invoked by light, colour and texture. One could say that rather than explicitly instructing behaviour (as composition, orientation and signage do), the use of largely immaterial effects as a design medium is an effort to activate the emotional being. Which of these imprints a more lasting image in your memory: an efficient walk across town, during which the office blocks, shop fronts, pavements, park edges and streets all defer quietly to a singular strategy of functionality and overarching rationality; or a stroll, along which the eye experiences a continuum of striking colours, curious textures and dramatic light schemes, all fulfiling the requisite needs of the cityscape yet each challenging the visitor to see with fresh eyes?

The viewer's expectations are guided by light, colour and texture. If a garden were made entirely out of bright red materials there would be certain intuitive responses. If we were to walk through a city plaza at night and suddenly all the streetlights went off, an alarm would sound within our heads, as the character of the space suddenly skews from calm to unsafe. An expanse of mowed turf is perceived quite differently from a rustling field of waist-high grasses. As we encounter a landscape – be it urban or intimate – our emotional projections of use and meaning are steered by such immediate indicators as light, colour and texture.

Sensory perception is active, not passive, and thereby designers who purposefully (and skillfully) incorporate colours with which we identify feelings, tactile materials, aromas and distinguishing sounds capture the visitor's attention from the moment the space is discovered. Experience of place is, in Edward T. Hall's words, 'a transaction between man and his environment in which both participate'[4]. Hall also notes that the palaeolithic cave artist, and similarly a young child, tended to be 'only dimly aware that this world could be experienced as separate from himself'. For the purposes of this discussion, I will add modern man and woman to this classification. What is it that differentiates knowledge of self from that of place? First and foremost we notice aspects of a site that serve our needs directly, for example, how do I walk from here to there? What time of day is the fountain active? Who is sitting on my favourite bench? Second, as we become increasingly familiar with a place and its purported purpose, additional layers of meaning and use come forth that do not stem directly from our personal interest: the violet hue of the iris beds in blossom, the reflection of city lights and the sun's arc on a canal, the way rain water flows through gravel and seeps into a retention marsh, the sound of heels clamouring up and down stone steps at rush hour.

LIGHT
The power of light lies in the presence of darkness. In garden design, light is used primarily in two manners: to create architectural form, in which case light is a critical means to an end but is not a salient feature; or to illuminate, either for theatrical effect or as functional lighting. It stands to reason that in radical gardens light is used in bold strokes and highlights unexpected elements. Light is an exciting medium, but it is intangible – lighting can be highly controlled, yet ever-changing. Cast in solid form, as in Ken Smith's Glowing Topiary Garden in New York (p. 14), or applied as an invisible force that heightens the fluid poetics of water, as in Barbara Hunt's 1997 installation for Hampton Court Palace Flower Show (p. 16), light is an essential tool of garden architecture.

1 Le Corbusier. Towards a New
Architecture (New York: Praeger, 1970).
2 Webster's New World College Dictionary
(fourth edition).
3 Hunt, John Dixon. 'Land, Art, Land Art
& Landscape Architecture'. Between
Landscape Architecture and Land Art, Udo
Weilacher (Basel: Birkhauser, 1996): 6.
4 Hall, Edward T. The Hidden Dimension
(New York: Doubleday Anchor, 1966): 82.
5 Bennett, Alan. 'Colour'. The Guardian
Weekend (London, 11 December 1999): 35.

In some projects light is used as a means to gain objectivity: exactly where, when, in what setting does the work exist? Illumination is a clarifying agent in the service of reality. Yet in other instances, the essence of light is abstraction and the eye plays a game with the revealed space/object relationship. The detailing of light effects can simultaneously expose the simplicity and the extravagance found within one site.

If a corollary of illumination is reflection, then certainly the reciprocate is shadow. Several designers featured in this chapter examine the relationship between light and shadow, treating each as a type of mutable form that either creates a changing pattern or cyclically defines a spatial experience. In the Swamp Garden in South Carolina (p. 18), designed by Adriaan Geuze of West 8 for the 1997 Spoleto Arts Festival, sunlight is incorporated by means of two mechanisms. First, a wire framework of hanging Spanish moss attracts the sun's rays and forms amorphous silhouettes that appear to be a merging of solid cypress trunks and the swamp's liquid surface. Second, the moss curtains and boardwalk delineate a particular section of the swamp, thereby drawing attention to the water's surface. Quotidian reflections in this area, by being framed, are elevated to an ensconced, jewel-like status.

COLOUR

Colour is applied to inanimate objects to rouse response and identification. It is also a means of conveying information, both cultural and biological, about a place, object or grouping of objects. Some of the projects in this chapter, such as Mario Schjetnan's Casa Malinalco gardens in Mexico (p. 30), showcase nature's brilliant hues – the scattered petals of potted perennials, a cerulean backdrop – alongside complementary shades of paint on enclosing walls to produce a unified, three-dimensional composition. The eye does not distinguish between man's brush stroke and nature's pigmentation: the two sources are rendered unimportant by the harmony and elevation of the effect as a whole. The gardens hold few objects, emphasizing the dominance of the interplay between colour, light and texture.

Schjetnan uses deeply saturated colour to establish physical nuances and to make reference to the spiritual/ mythological aspects of modern space. In contrast, Mark Rios presents a muted tapestry of earth tones in his selection of grasses for a private residence in Southern California (p. 26). Here, colour is less objectified and becomes instead a neutral field that holds the design together at the shore of a vast landscape. English playwright Alan Bennett once commented on the power of a contiguous – although not necessarily regularized – colour scheme versus sharply contrasting tones. He appreciates 'the edge of colours: green when it's about to become yellow, red on the verge of orange'. Bennett points to this as a 'general principle going way beyond art or decoration .... People of widely differing views, contrasting colours, if you like, are less interesting to listen to than people whose views are different but quite close together .... I prefer to deal with the edges of emotions rather than their extremes, irritation rather than anger, melancholy rather than grief.' His instinct is 'for adjacence, ambiguity and being in two minds'.[5]

TEXTURE

Sometimes texture is about tactility, sometimes about topography. In either case, texturing concerns the conscious perception of a surface (even when that surface is a result of underlying forces). The critical factor is scale: is the scheme a rich mixture of grains, veneers and modules with which the human eye and hand physically interact; or does the site's contouring imply superhuman movement and gesture?

At Keith Wagner's Vermont residence (p. 28), building materials and plants are chosen specifically for textural (and contextual) juxtapositions: rough stone against delicate fern fronds; a mounded moss floor balances the swooping stone wall. Wagner's plant selection catches you by surprise: the gently undulating mass of Scottish moss reads as a carpet and imparts a sense of control typically associated with interior space. At the other end of the spectrum, at the San Diego Children's Pond and Park (p. 34), Peter Walker and Partners planted bright flowers in raised earthen discs and installed a grid of evergreens that act as a counterpoint to the surrounding urban texture. Close up, the composition reads as a figure/ground study; at a distance, as distinct textures within the city fabric.

In this way, we begin to understand that our role in a designed landscape is dichotomized; we project our needs onto a site and we are influenced by a site's constitution. It is at this point that the masterful implementation of light, colour and texture can influence the visitor's impressions, conduct and memory.

SHADES OF ALLUSION
Glowing Topiary Garden
Liberty Plaza, New York City, US, 1997, Ken Smith Landscape Architect

Created in collaboration with lighting designer Jim Conti, the two-month garden installation celebrates the winter solstice in the heart of New York's Financial District. The design structure reflects in part the underlying formality of the site – an open city block with gridded trees (see pp. 10–11) accented by an adjacent Isamu Noguchi cube sculpture – and in part the desire to hide an allée of 1970s-style 'lollipop' streetlights. Sixteen 'topiary lanterns' constructed from galvanized-steel-pipe framing and translucent vinyl awning, each 16 feet (4.9 metres) high with a base diameter of 8 feet (2.4 metres), were placed over the existing lights.

A singular 24-foot-high (7.3 metres) topiary cone anchors the plaza's centre and reaches into barren tree branches. Electronic sound-emitting devices and multicoloured fluorescent lighting enliven each cone. Two hundred and fifty wind chimes hang in the trees, further paganizing the fast-paced Financial District by bringing 'light, mystery, and pleasure to the shortest days of the year'.

Smith responds to 'the conceptual problems of creating landscape in the urban space of contemporary society' by synthesizing French topiary techniques and Japanese garden influences into unambiguous geometric forms. His design explores ideas of ambient space and makes the point that today's most provocative landscapes are often reinterpretations of traditional civic places. The use of light and sound reworks expectations of the public plaza, elevating the typically passive pedestrian zone by conjuring abstracted symbols of celebration and spirituality during the holiday season.

The emotive power of landscape, at times underestimated, is fully exploited by Smith and Conti in the Glowing Topiary Garden. The project addresses issues of urban experience, of illumination as art, of the spatial power of simple geometries and of the utility of ephemeral landscape installations as opposed to permanent works in the public realm.

OF FLOWING GLASS AND GLOWING GRASS
Water Moods Garden
Hampton Court Palace Flower Show, UK, 1997, Barbara Hunt (Hunt Design)

'Glass grasses' appear alongside herbaceous plantings in Hunt's exploration of the differing characteristics of light and water. As visitors move through the installation, the mood shifts from sparkling to sombre, an allegory that is played out by the manipulation of liquidity, reflection and illumination. At the garden's centre is a raised pool with sheets of glass set at varying angles against the backdrop of a wall. Water is emitted from slits in the wall, pouring over the sheets and slipping into the pool in a silent performance that is dramatized by uplighting. The glass creates an almost invisible surface over which the water surges, seeming to flow suspended in the air.

In Hunt's scheme, plant materials, paving and concrete landscape structures – typical focal points within gardens – are foils that highlight the interplay of light, glass and water. Described by the designer as a contemporary water garden of tranquillity and peace, the innovative aspects of the design are best understood in relation to the surrounding context of the historic flower show. It is the unique detailing and a curiosity about micro-scale dialogues – the definition of a single leaf's silhouette against a plane of moving water, the potential interpretation of glowing glass rods as botanical hyperbole – that draw the eye.

REFRACTION AND REFLECTION
Swamp Garden
Charleston, South Carolina, US, 1997, West 8 Landscape Architects

When invited to participate in the 1997 Spoleto Arts Festival, landscape architect Adriaan Geuze and colleagues (Cyrus B. Clark, Marnix Vink, Trevor Bullen) avoided faux regionalism/contextualism – approaches that rely on current fashions and that are particularly alluring to those unfamiliar with the local scene. Instead, in keeping with the festival's theme of 'Human/Nature: Art and Landscape in Charleston and the Low Country', the team concentrated on the peculiarities of their chosen site to develop a comprehensive scheme that is not mired in an arbitrary moment in time. It is a strategy that encompasses evolution of site and surroundings, materially and culturally. It incorporates memory – collective and individual – but without the lacquer of nostalgic interpretation.

The Swamp Garden is created by a rectangular structure of steel poles interconnected by steel wires, placed in and delineating a particular section of the delightfully spectral low-country waterland. Spanish moss is draped over the wires, forming ultra-light wavy walls that contrast with the solid stance of the captured cypress trunks. In this open-air chamber, the swamp's constant modulations in atmosphere – from the sun's reflection to rings of raindrops to the glowering moon – are framed and implicitly prioritized.

A wood boardwalk carries visitors from terra firma out over the water, through the airy curtain of moss and along the inside edge of the swamp room. A platform allows boats to dock within the rectangle and passengers to access the boardwalk. Two benches, made from reclaimed cypress trunks found on site, are the ideal spot from which to observe 'the surreal isolation', turtles and the occasional alligator.

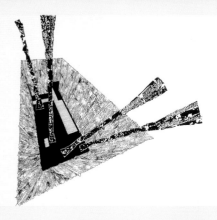

RECONSIDERING URBAN INFRASTRUCTURE
Washington State Convention and Trade Center Atrium and Lobby
Seattle, US, 1992, Danadjieva & Koenig Associates

An extension of the celebrated Freeway Park in Seattle, Angela Danadjieva's scheme for the 727,000-square-foot (67,500 square metres) atrium and lobby stems from her conviction that 'we cannot afford to have only one use of urban space'. The tri-storey atrium welcomes visitors to conference and convention facilities, retail shops, offices, a series of interior plazas used for public gatherings, parking and access to three city streets. All this, remarkably, occupies a multi-level bridge structure that sits atop twelve busy lanes of Interstate 5 in downtown Seattle.

Seemingly carved in concrete layers out of a futuristic bedrock, the interior public space echoes the language of its ground-breaking antecedent Freeway Park. A 2-acre (0.8 hectares) garden plaza connects the old and the new, permitting an uninterrupted stretch of green to flow horizontally and vertically through this sector of the city. It is the very first instance of an interior park, complete with fountains, spanning a major highway. It is difficult to tell where architecture ends and nature begins. Or, which part is urban infrastructure and which part is civic amenity. That is no mistake – Danadjieva and her colleagues set out to blur the lines of distinction in a manner that allows the public spaces an intense degree of multi-tasking. →

→ To decrease loading and construction cost, Danadjieva designed the interior concrete walls as hollow structures, using shotcrete applications (sprayed-on concrete), precast panels and poured-in-place concrete. Despite three different installation methods, the result presents a unified texture. Lower decks are dedicated to vehicular circulation and parking, upper levels to a vibrant pedestrian environment. Surrounded by waterfalls and abundant vegetation that spill over concrete walls (which reflect Northwest Basalt formations), people might have a sneaking suspicion that they have entered a rainforest diorama. Yet the force of the creation – the magnitude of the concrete landscape and the earnest joy expressed in the success of the interior plantings – powers the landscape far beyond a city-dweller's pallid rendition of nature. It does not matter which illuminations and textures are natural and which are man-made; here the two sources artfully coexist in a dramatic new urban prototype.

MULTIMEDIA IN THE GARDEN
The Hanging Garden of Golders Green
London, UK, 1991, Paul Cooper

A dark damp plot surrounded by conifers in London's Golders Green neighbourhood has been transformed by designer Paul Cooper into 'an oasis of light and colour'. A stainless-steel and glass waterfall animates the heart of the site and sets the scene for a busy interplay of materials, textures, lighting and video effects. The theatrical character of the residential garden is reinforced by the fact that it is raised 12 feet (3.7 metres) above ground level on wood decking. Described by Cooper as a 'multi-level, multi-media, multi-purpose and multi-experience garden', the space defies immediate identification. One must negotiate the various levels and visit the site during the day and at night to grasp the rich mix of effects.

Cooper selected low-maintenance plantings to fill boxes that double as walls and furniture in the outdoor media room. Greenery tumbles over sides and from one level to the next, echoing the textural flow of the custom-crafted waterfall of convulsing metal. Solid vertical surfaces contrast with Cooper's non-standard railings, which themselves play dual roles as a safeguarding exostructure and as sculptural screens. The garden is fully engineered for night-time use: atmospheric flexibility includes soft ambient illumination for intimate gatherings and video panels to show films or to project still images into the space. According to Cooper, 'Special effects extend the dimensions of the garden'.

[below, left] **CULTIVATING ATMOSPHERE**
A Fantasy Garden
London, UK, 1998, Paul Cooper
In Muswell Hill, Cooper again sets the stage with various
special effects. Coloured lights, primitive stone walls
with surprises hidden in niches, custom-made metal
trellis-work, active water and attitude come together to
create a residential garden that is anything but a backdrop.

[below, middle] **THE ABSENCE OF SOLID GROUND**
Floating Garden
Chelsea Flower Show, UK, 1997, Paul Cooper
Plants and people rest or walk on water in this site bite that
incorporates plant arrangements, water and wood. Cooper
selected plant species to achieve specific contrasts of shape
and texture, all showcased in a multi-tiered presentation.

[below, right] **DIALOGUE OF SHAPE AND TEXTURE**
Garden for Torrens
Weybridge, UK, 1993, Paul Cooper
Working alongside horticulturalist Jo Mathews, Cooper
was given the task of designing a garden in the modern
idiom that would also relate to the clients' house dating
from the 1930s. The pair responded by fashioning an intricate
scheme in which every surface matters, from paving to
painted timber frames that focus lines of vision. One
reviewer commented that 'textures rub and jar against
each other – grass, paving, cobbles, gravel, slate, concrete
and brick – to the effect of accentuating individual qualities
of each without fragmenting the composition'.

As we encounter a garden our
emotional projections of its use
and meaning are steered by
such immediate indicators as
light, colour and texture.

CONTEXT AMPLIFIED
Private Residence
California, US, 1997, Rios Associates

Simple, powerful, massive gestures: these are strategies that landscape architect Mark Rios employs in many of his garden and site designs. 'A reduced palette with mono-chromatic masses gives the landscape its own weight,' explains Rios. The concept of scale is critical to the project shown here; the seemingly all-encompassing grasses have a boldness that balances the sizeable house against the sloping terrain. A severe landscape solution, in a sense, but one that holds its own. The kinetic energy of each stalk, when read as a rippling whole, creates a cloudlike impression: perhaps there is no solid ground beneath the millions of bladed and tufted leaves.

One source of inspiration came from the site's context – the property overlooks the Playa Vista marsh, a textured sea of native vegetation. The house and private land are visually connected to the marsh by a shared palette and the expansive scale. The plant list includes Pennisetum, Miscanthus, bamboo and many sedge and grass varieties, such as deer and gamma grasses. 'We see the work as abstracting nature in some ways,' says Rios, who likens the purity of other planting schemes he has developed for Los Angeles residences to a decompression chamber or a palette cleanser in comparison to architectural and contextual complexities.

FRESH CREATION BALANCES RENOVATION
Les Confines
**t-Rémy-de-Provence, France, 1993, Dominique
afourcade**

he 'tamed' shapes and colours of wild species and
ernacular materials found in the Mediterranean
egion are the building blocks for artist and garden
esigner Dominique Lafourcade's family compound
t Les Confines. It is an intrinsic reference to the
istory – ecological and cultural – of Provence that
rouses the eye, the nose and the sensation of a
istant memory.

The project began in 1990 as a collaboration
ith her husband, architect Bruno Lafourcade, on
he renovation of an eighteenth-century farmhouse
nd 25 acres (10 hectares) of flat wheat fields. The
afourcades wanted to 'create a garden out of
othing'. One of the first things they did was to
emove a decaying barn and install a pool in its

footprint. The pool is one node in the garden's water
circuit, a series of irrigation features – functional and
aesthetically evocative – that tap the precious water
table just 9 feet (2.7 metres) below ground. The circuit
is powered by a windmill, built by the couple, that
captures the consistent Mistral winds.

In the topiary garden adjacent to the pool, native
shrubs have been artfully shaped. Dominique
Lafourcade finds that the interplay of forms speaks a
language of its own. Bulbous evergreens, squared-off
hedge segments and conical cypress become a
menagerie somewhere between purposeful cultivation
and collective peculiarity. Elsewhere, the rigidity of
axial paths is relaxed by a heightened tactility as
vegetation and paving are textured by the artist's hand.

In radical gardens light
is used in bold strokes
and highlights
unexpected elements.

A BINDING THREAD OF LIGHT
Private Residence
Vermont, US, 1998, The Office of H. Keith Wagner

A trough of light links house and arrival court in the contemporary rural residence, a striking element that cuts through stone, moss and fern. Landscape architect Keith Wagner envisioned the 8-inch-wide (20 cm), recessed bar (shaped to reflect a vertical window cut into the house's façade) as a meta-gesture extending far into the surrounding forest. Ferns and other vegetation bordering the light trough have reflective qualities to strengthen the near-spiritual effect of the illuminated strip of forest floor.

The simple, luminous trough has a surprisingly powerful presence. Although it is neither the measured foot-candles of interior fixtures nor the filtered daylight of the woods, the glow belongs to both and easily serves as the essential link between the two. The condition took effort to achieve; Wagner and his associates laboured for months on mock-ups to reproduce exactly the same quality of light in the earth as emitted by the adjacent window. The final solution is a galvanized trough with micro-lights (protected by plastic tubing) set at 12-inch (30 cm) intervals. Light is diffused by textured Plexiglas and bounces off the sides of the trough. It is, in Wagner's words, 'a thread of light pulled down the façade and out into the garden'.

Wagner chooses common materials from the encompassing Vermont hill farms and forest lands, then applies them to the residential composition with deductive clarity. The resulting site is readily identifiable as upland forest, epitomized and abridged at the same time. 'We abstracted the basic site materials into a sculptural composition,' Wagner explains. 'It's a reduced palette chosen for subtle variations in hue and texture.' The subtle variations allow the star moves – the light trough, the site stone, the house itself – to stand out all the more. (See also pp. 74–75.)

IN THE ORCHARD
Casa Malinalco
Mexico, 1985, Mario Schjetnan

Amid gnarled trunks and fragrant air, architect and landscape architect Mario Schjetnan carved rooms for a house and garden from a venerable orchard in the historic valley of Malinalco. According to Schjetnan, the design is 'an exercise between the old constants of climate, architecture, landscape, and culture'. The climate (subtropical), the architecture (an L-shaped plan with living areas open to a central courtyard), the landscape (agricultural and semi-rural) and the culture (a synthesis of contemporary and ancient Mexican traditions, tinged with Spanish and Moroccan attitude), all culminate in spaces bursting with colour, light and texture.

The garden occupies three levels: the upper courtyard, adjacent to the main living quarters; the mid-level 'semi-wild' orchard of coffee, banana and mango trees; and the cobblestone-paved lower level, holding stables and services. The upper courtyard is described by Schjetnan as a space in which 'all elements of nature interplay to create a microcosm: water, soil, plants, fire, and sky, as well as birds and a few squirrels'. The north-south axis of the courtyard is marked by a thin channel of water linking a fountain at one end to a stone-carved water mirror at the other end. Grey- and rainwater are recycled, in part through these features, and fed into the orchard.

[right] **MAVERICK SEDGE IN THE CORPORATE REALM**
Terraces at Canary Wharf
London, UK, 1998, J+L Gibbons Landscape

'This project was challenging both in terms of programme and schedule,' states landscape architect Johanna Gibbons. Given just two months to design and implement a scheme for bi-level roof terraces, the firm devised a textured tapestry as a visual foreground for extensive dockland views from the office windows. The simple and geometric 'parterres' relate to the 'clear-cut modern lines and articulation of the architecture'. Western red-cedar planks frame pre-grown mats of sedum and herbs, selected for their low maintenance and hardiness against wind turbulence, but also for their immediate visual impact and ongoing seasonal interest. Crucial to the project, however, is the 'maverick element' of a wild vegetal texture with a degree of unpredictability regarding the final balance of plant species.

[middle right] **MASSAGING LAND, LIGHT AND SHADOW**
Mnemonic River
Massachusetts, US, 1985, Janis Hall

Janis Hall describes her work as 'somewhere between environmental art, landscape architecture, and architecture'. The approach is readily apparent in the 10-acre (4 hectares) coastal site of Mnemonic River; a quietly forceful residential design that blends topographic movement with a profound understanding of the interplay between sunlight and shadow. There is a timeless quality to the cycle of daylight and the seasons along seashores, an all-pervasive essence that Hall taps into when she shapes earthforms and plantings to induce an impression of light and land flowing together toward the sea.

[below] **SHAVING SHAPE, TELLING TEXTURE**
La Florida Estate
Spain, 1986, Fernando Caruncho

Sculpted shrubs – Escallonia macrantha – surround the deck of the swimming pool in landscape architect Fernando Caruncho's design for La Florida Estate. Although growth is shaped and controlled over time, as in the tradition of topiary, the massing suggests a more amorphous being that serves as a signified background rather than as an object. The proportional scale of texturing truly determines a site's character, as evidenced by comparing the varying scales depicted here.

LIQUID MEASURE
Le Carrousel d'Eau
Festival International des Jardins, Chaumont-sur-Loire, France, 1997, Michele Elsair & Jean-Pierre Delettre

Architect Michele Elsair and 'inventor of strange machines' Jean-Pierre Delettre conceived and constructed 'Le Carrousel d'Eau', an entry in the 1997 annual festival of contemporary gardens held in Chaumont-sur-Loire. Reverberation and reflectivity are the chief concerns of the garden installation, and there is a level of complexity in the machinery devised by Delettre to achieve these qualities. Suspended cables support a series of dividers that section the scheme into water aisles, each of which showcases a different engineered surface effect from concentric circles of water to a hand-operated ferry that traces its own wake, and from sheets of smooth water to bubbles rising from the pool's depths and bursting at its surface. Black water – the pool is lined with ebony to resemble dark ponds carpeted with rotting leaves – is 'a mirror of the changing sky; a barometrical mirror, blue if the sky is blue, silvered and rippled by the breeze if overcast'. Dense planting frames the carousel with butterbur, ligularia, hosta, duckweed, water lettuce and water hyacinth.

ORDERING PLAY IN THE PARK
Children's Pond and Park
San Diego, US, 1996, Peter Walker and Partners

In sun-saturated Southern California, a sexy salty colour palette is noticeable in the oceanside city of San Diego. The landscape architecture firm Peter Walker and Partners picked up on this in their design for a pond and park in the midst of downtown's redevelopment area. A brilliant-blue central pool and hot-pink ice-plant mounds stand out against a generally verdant backdrop. In turn, allées of Italian cypress, a ring of Mexican fan palms and sodded turf hillocks interspersed with Canary Island pines are offset by a ground plane of neutral, decomposed granite and patterned paving.

As an extension and a focal point of the city's waterfront promenade, the pond and park also relate to the neighbouring Horton Plaza, Convention Center and Children's Museum. Playful landforms and undeniable spatial clarity easily coexist. The scheme's bold geometry and urban scale (rail systems traverse the 200-foot-diameter [61 metres] pool without distracting from the whole) read from the distance as an idealized version of

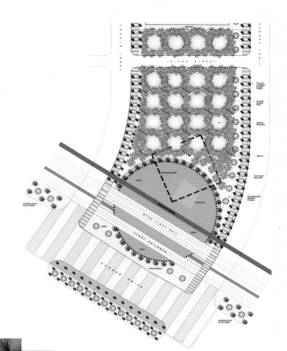

the city. It is almost like a child's simplified representation of the cityscape, cheerfully hand-coloured with favourite crayons, skillfully keeping within the lines.

San Diego Children's Pond and Park is described by the firm as 'a (relatively) low-budget adventure-play landscape' that offers visitors 'shade, greenery, and the coolness of water', while also showcasing 'the dynamic side of San Diego, with its saturated colors and elemental shapes'. In his book Peter Walker: Minimalist Gardens (Washington, DC: Spacemaker Press, 1997), Walker discusses fragmentation of the contemporary landscape and notes that 'distinguishing landscape units such as the Los Angeles Basin, the Island of Manhattan, and the Charles River Basin in Boston ... have been visually weakened' by elements of industrial society. Perhaps our urban structures have also been weakened over time and landscape design such as this will play a role in re-establishing an overall sense of order and connection to the greater body.

Rainbird sprinkler heads cast an array of animating effects on the pool's surface, from linear shadow patterns to puckered sunlight as drops scatter on the water.

Plane Movement

The landscape we see in the built world is a veneer. What we consider solid ground is actually a contrived set of impressions and solutions.

As [the garden artist] takes hold of earth, plants, and water, the materials unique to his art, let him only beware lest he destroy through his act of possession the genius of that which he has sought to possess. **Elizabeth Kassler**[1]

Designers and engineers texture the ground plane with earthwork, plantings, or hardscape to achieve various effects. For example, a rolling formation of ripples or undulations implies a sense of movement on what we might traditionally understand to be an inert mass. The result is engaging, but disorienting; by adjusting one element in the frame of our stage – earth and sky – radical designers cause us to re-examine just where we stand.

The human eye is drawn to contrast. Changes in size, colour and texture are a staple of almost every artistic endeavour. To be effective, the use of contrast must be strong: the elements in question must be featured in sufficient amounts to be noticed and to hold their own against each other. A grove of birch or beech trees is distinctive because it differs from the surrounding forest. A stretch of cresting sand dunes acts as the seam that joins sea and land. The result must be pure and consistent to draw the eye and to make a statement. The radical landscapes shown here use variations in landform and texture – on a scale ranging from the minute to the grand – to create contrast and movement.

Artist and architect Maya Lin's study of fluid dynamics provided the inspiration for the Wave Field at the University of Michigan (p. 42). Not only does Lin create unfamiliar conditions by ascribing the attributes of water to a stretch of turf, but she exaggerates the novelty by inviting the viewer to walk through the Wave Field. The repetitive wave forms give the impression of liquidity, particularly from a distance, and thus as one enters the sculpted ground the effect of 'walking on water' is evinced. By altering the distinction between two knowns – the instability of water surface and the solidity of terra firma – Lin pushes the art of built landscape past its functional framework, beyond the model of nature and into the realm of purposefully provocative media.

This state is more easily achieved within a limited site, like the courtyard in which the Wave Field is located. On a larger scale, the play of earthwork, plantings or other design elements that deliver a sense of plane movement is significantly more complex, requiring the visitor to acknowledge multiple sets of circumstances before fully comprehending the underlying connection to context or fulfilment of programme.

For example, at West 8 Landscape Architects' Interpolis Garden (p. 44) a 'loose pattern of tectonic shifts' is intended to convey a 'strong, constantly changing sense of perspective'[2]. The tectonic activity is multifold; it is expressed with varying materials and, depending on placement, weaves into the site's functional identity (a corporate garden) on several levels. On the largest scale, the grass surface that serves as the garden's base is sliced into a series of horizontally overlapping wedges, divided by walkways and punctuated by several elongated, trapezoidal lily pools. The turf wedges are denaturalized – i.e., the impression of a grassy field is purposefully avoided – by concrete retaining edges that double as seats for company employees. While hoping to impart a constant sense of terrestrial movement (as opposed to the fluid dynamics model), from the grand concept of a faulted shifting ground plane down to such details as loose, wood-chip pathways and a shingled slate apron along the adjacent office headquarters, programmatic and aesthetic priorities are weighed equally. Therefore, despite the vivid visual impact of a crustal ground plane, the garden's components are easily categorized into entry sequence, circulation diagram and site amenities that address both the day-to-day needs of employees and the cultivation of corporate identity.

In the Waterland project (p. 46), Janis Hall employs plane movement to relate to the natural setting, using it as a topographic language rather than as a means for distortion. Hall first worked with a clay maquette before directing bulldozers in the field; she moved from massaging a site model with thumb and fingers to waving arms at piles of dirt. As apparent in Fletcher Steele's 1938 contour-shaping at Naumkeag (Massachusetts), and showing evidence of Hall's past work with landscape architect A. E. Bye, the undulating berms of Waterland echo distant ridgelines and parallel the silhouette of bordering wind rows. It may be difficult to distinguish the pre-existing from the man-made ground plane in projects such as this, but that is a testament to the finesse with which designers observe and respond to site conditions with, in Hall's words, 'quiet, bold moves'.

By nature of its surface variation, the art of plane movement often relies upon light and shadow to produce interesting effects. It is notoriously difficult to capture on film the experience of movement and perception of depth in the landscape. The time of day or artificial lighting is crucial; even then, it is likely that some degree of texture and depth will be lost against the background and that the landscape will appear flattened.

As with many aspects of art and architecture, the complexity of the forms must relate directly to the scale of the moves in landscape architecture. It will not do to have intricate rippling patterns, carved earthworks or a hectic composition of topiary forms if the adjacent buildings, the outlying landscape, or the overall site parameters are diminutive. It is critical to attune the design objectives with the spatial capacity of the site. At Studio on Site's Natori Cultural Hall in Japan (p. 50), a very simple field of gently undulating mowed grass is accentuated by lines of square-cut stone set flush with the turf surface. No more and no less is needed – the designers define the park's essence and reach outward to neighbouring land. Yet the plane movement would be almost undetectable if not for the white stones that trace the grade. In the firm's project brochure, it is pointed out that earthwork, as one component of a greater whole, 'acts as a catalyst to induce movement'. Studio on Site also discusses the technical considerations of plane movement, 'Earthworks are not simply a matter of regulating space by the shapes that are apparent on the surface of the land. In fact it is those invisible things such as methods of drainage, the composition of soil and the structure of the land below the surface that in reality decide the quality of the spaces on the face of the site.'[3]

In describing Parque del Torrent Ballester (p. 53), architect Arturo Frediani Sarfati explains that the traditional city park is 'seen through the eyes of the Romantic', where the landscape adheres to a vision of nature bisected by pathways so that the observer does not truly interact with the setting. In contrast, the Parque del Torrent Ballester is a conglomeration of open spaces, an overlapping arrangement of paved and green areas unfettered by pathways, intersections, promenades and squares. The park is non-hierarchical, routes will be established over time by those who use the place. Neither man nor nature dominates; it is a creation that takes into consideration the dynamism of human beings, nature's cycles and the city's patterns of growth. It is the transfer of 'urban textures onto open spaces in an appropriate scale' that, depending on how it is understood and shaped by many ungovernable forces, will develop unity over time.

The form of the ground plane can carry potent symbolism within a landscape. From the spiritual earthworks of ancient civilizations to the masterfully engineered slopes and water channels of the golden age of Italian and French garden design, to the earth artists who emerged in the late1960s in America, man has shaped the land to communicate power and his position within a greater realm, be it cosmic, spiritual, political or social. The pastoral impulse of the English garden tradition, for example, is evident in Frederick Law Olmsted's Central Park in New York, where one can read the intended land use in the gentle topographic differences in the various areas of the park: from wooded glen to rocky knoll, from shady dell to open meadow, the park re-creates an entire regional experience by meticulous contouring and schematic plantings.

This chronology of artful manipulation of the earth's surface indicates that today's radical garden designers who work in the medium of topography are hardly unique. Perhaps what distinguishes the work shown in this chapter is the desire to explore the impossible attributes of the solid ground plane: fluidity, turbulence, formlessness, disconnection from underlying layers. Or the wish to succinctly articulate specific points within a complex environment. Sometimes the suggestion of something is stronger than the actual thing because one must be engaged to perceive and use the imagination to fill in the gaps.[4] Certainly, these designers find that plane movement is a multifaceted tool.

1 Kassler, Elizabeth. Modern Gardens and the Landscape (New York: Museum of Modern Art, 1964).
2 Project statement from West 8 Landscape Architects.
3 Statement from Studio on Site brochure.
4 Based on a statement by Janis Hall in 'Stone's Flow'. Landscape Architecture. Alicia Rodriguez (August 1999): 26.

The artful manipulation of the earth's surface, through changes in size, colour and texture, creates an engaged landscape.

THE FLUID DYNAMICS OF TERRA FIRMA
Wave Field
University of Michigan, Ann Arbor, US, 1995, Maya Lin Studio

Topographic manipulation of the ground plane is a hallmark of contemporary land design. At the University of Michigan's new FXB Aerospace Engineering Building, artist and architect Maya Lin continues her exploration in topology and landscape with Wave Field, an outdoor earthwork that suggests unusual tectonic possibilities for a traditional university yard.

In researching the site and programme, Lin was inspired by readings in aero- and fluid dynamics. The resulting site parti is a series of precisely shaped, sodded berms that translate concepts of fluidity and turbulence resistance onto a relatively inert surface. The visual implication is of endless motion, a trompe-l'oeil that defies our typical perception of solid ground.

Lin created clay and sand models to work out the three-dimensional nature of the contouring – a critical aspect of the sculpture's success because the waves' height and base measurements imitate the physical realities of fluid motion. The regularity of the pattern was altered to enforce the impression of fluidity: what appears as a consistent parallelogram grid is distorted so that the grid spreads out from one corner. A custom-made sandy-soil mix ensures that the waves hold their shape and allows quick drainage. The stature of the landforms encourages visitors to wander through and even sit on the grassy waves. From the site's perimeter and from classrooms above, the appearance of 'endless motion' morphs with the sun's angles.

43

ECTONICS TAKES HOLD
nterpolis Garden
ilburg, The Netherlands, 1998, West 8 Landscape Architects

ables of water, chunky pathways and an apron of layered slate labs comprise a 5-acre (2 hectares) corporate garden for the nterpolis headquarters. Landscape architect Adriaan Geuze and olleagues set out to create 'a calm and introverted world' to balance he sizeable adjoining office building (see pp. 38–39). However, the ectilinear site elements, seeming in plan to slip past each other as hismatched pieces in the wrong puzzle, are a far cry from traditional xpectations of a soothing composition. There is no apparent ordering rinciple in the two-dimensional version of the scheme. Yet within the arden, sitting beside gently glittering pools and strolling mulched valkways separated from the city streets by a hedge-backed steel ence, the hands-on experience is one of serenity (in comparison o the surrounding urban and corporate realms).

A general pattern of horizontal overlap in 'stage-like, non-parallel rrangements' is meant to resemble tectonic plate movement and o offer a 'strong, constantly changing sense of perspective'. This hifting, drifting effect is at odds with the standardized urban context, et it skillfully serves the site's functional mandate of corporate oasis. he garden's grass surface is overlaid with a cut-out path system and vedge-shaped lily and frog ponds. The water platforms and turf infill re ironic twists on the pastoral scenery found in many corporate arks, in fact, appropriately Dutch twists, in a nation of thoroughly ngineered water and land ecologies.

At the north side of the quadrangular site, a slate apron provides pedestal for the headquarters. Here, the theme of tectonic activity ccurs on a smaller scale: the slate covering is fractured into verlapping shingles that catch light and shadow. In the spring, nagnolia trees drop fleshy petals onto the sharp stone surface. wood bridge climbs over the slate yard to lead office workers into he garden's interior. Douglas firs, planted in loose clusters across he site, mediate between the surrounding buildings and the strong raphic quality of the ground plane. Employees are invited to work n the garden on their laptop computers.

Hall produces near-haunting effects of light and volume by carving the land into sinuous contours.

ROLLING TERRAIN CAPTURES WATER AND LIGHT
Waterland
Northwest Connecticut, US, 1987, Janis Hall

Shaping a clay model by hand, then directing a bulldozer to translate the same rolling forms onto a vast landscape might be a daunting task for someone other than Janis Hall. 'It's the same thing really, just a change in scale,' she says. A student of both Isamu Noguchi and A. E. Bye, Hall began her career as a sculptor of objects, but then moved on to more spatially oriented work. At the 10-acre (4 hectares) Waterland residential site, foregrounds echo distant views and sculpted fields gesture to far hills and hedgerows, recalling portions of Fletcher Steele's 1938 earthwork at Naumkeag in Massachusetts.

Although Hall's landscapes are highly crafted, they are not purely self-referential. Her palette – 'earth, air, water, and life' – and the grading and planting plans attempt to weave into the existing environmental character of the site and its boundaries. At Waterland, Hall let the dramatic adjacency of high and low points in the glaciated terrain inform her topographical moves. Getting the right scale to the natural landforms was essential: the manipulation of the earth amplifies perception – 'it's like seeing the ocean,' she says. Spare, graceful and powerful, the results of Hall's creative process bring to mind the careful approach of Shaker woodworkers – both develop an intimate understanding of their materials and the specifics of place. The site plan (with north to the top) depicts the flowing contours that give shape to Waterland.

GROWING UP IN THE BODY POLITIC
European Parliament Garden
Strasbourg, France, Desvigne + Dalnoky

A narrow interior street, illuminated from above, runs through the body of the European Parliament building. Less than 23 feet (7 metres) wide, nearly 656 feet (200 metres) long and 98 feet (30 metres) high, the enclosed avenue is viewed from adjacent glassed offices and corridors. Fearing that trees would be out of scale in the long, linear space, landscape architects Michel Desvigne and Christine Dalnoky proposed a 'garden of vines' – not delicate, floral species, but junglelike vine cords and philodendrons sporting lush foliage.

The cables, which echo the building's structural system, guide the vines as they reach toward the nourishing skylight, and are flanked by white fibre-optic lines and small hoses that spray a fine mist onto the plantings. According to the design team, 'the plants live in their original state', while the gardener grows in artifice.

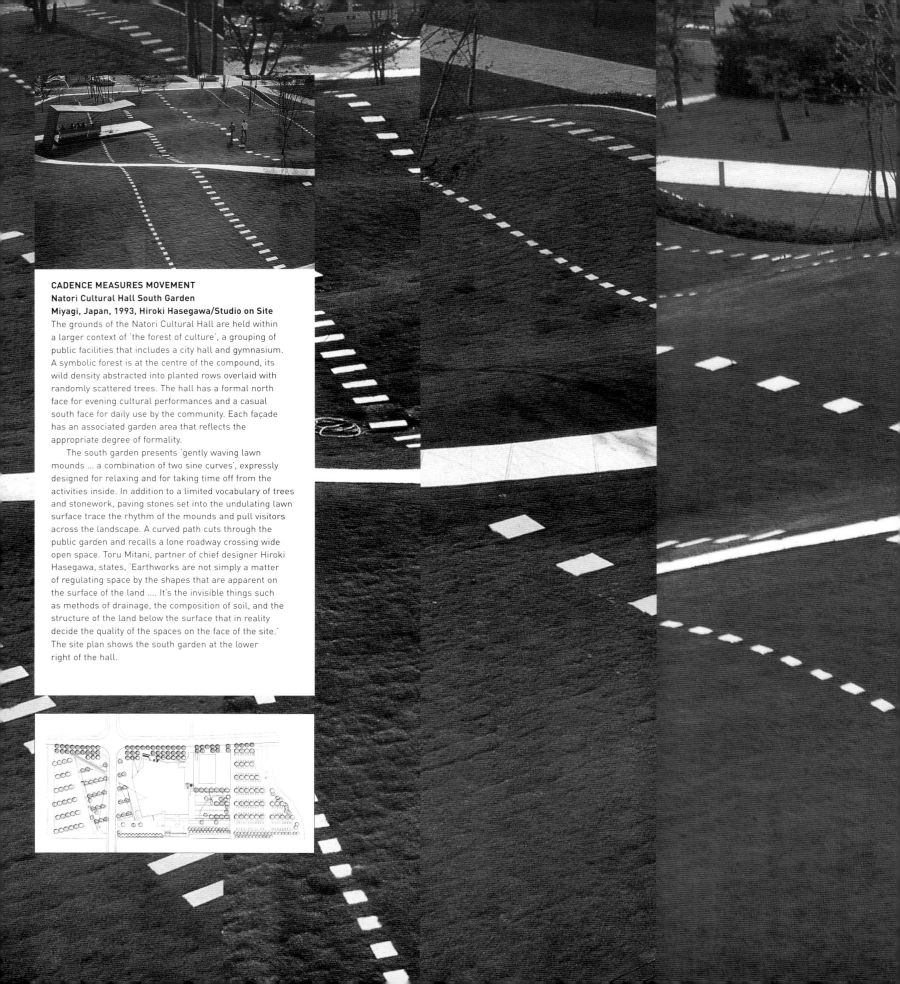

CADENCE MEASURES MOVEMENT
Natori Cultural Hall South Garden
Miyagi, Japan, 1993, Hiroki Hasegawa/Studio on Site

The grounds of the Natori Cultural Hall are held within a larger context of 'the forest of culture', a grouping of public facilities that includes a city hall and gymnasium. A symbolic forest is at the centre of the compound, its wild density abstracted into planted rows overlaid with randomly scattered trees. The hall has a formal north face for evening cultural performances and a casual south face for daily use by the community. Each façade has an associated garden area that reflects the appropriate degree of formality.

The south garden presents 'gently waving lawn mounds ... a combination of two sine curves', expressly designed for relaxing and for taking time off from the activities inside. In addition to a limited vocabulary of trees and stonework, paving stones set into the undulating lawn surface trace the rhythm of the mounds and pull visitors across the landscape. A curved path cuts through the public garden and recalls a lone roadway crossing wide open space. Toru Mitani, partner of chief designer Hiroki Hasegawa, states, 'Earthworks are not simply a matter of regulating space by the shapes that are apparent on the surface of the land .... It's the invisible things such as methods of drainage, the composition of soil, and the structure of the land below the surface that in reality decide the quality of the spaces on the face of the site.' The site plan shows the south garden at the lower right of the hall.

TOPOLOGICAL INSTABILITIES
Water Garden
Columbus, Ohio, US, 1997, Reiser + Umemoto, Jeffrey Kipnis, David Ruy

'Land carving' is the term that Nanako Umemoto applies to the design process for the Water Garden, a collaborative project with partner Jesse Reiser, Jeffrey Kipnis and David Ruy. 'It is a poignant garden,' describes Kipnis, whose residence in Columbus, Ohio serves as the testing ground for some of the team's creative output. The official project statement elaborates, 'Nature is less a "creation" to be speculated on than an inventive and modifiable matrix of material becomings'.

The Water Garden's vital media are water, soil, plant material and chemical salts. 'Unstable configurations' and 'local transformations' (warps, dimples, folds) built into the concrete substrate induce events in the 'flow space' above – primarily, discontinuities in the evolution of the vital media. The topography of the substrate, while it does not completely control or predict biological behaviour, diagrams potential instabilities and triggers interaction and interruption within the flow space. This link between inert geometric form and patterns of growth can be encouraged, even mapped. The result? Perhaps: 'In literal and instrumental fashion, multiform gradients in the geometry excite gradients of growth inherent in the Water Garden and yield a prodigious, if only partially manageable, field of blooms.'

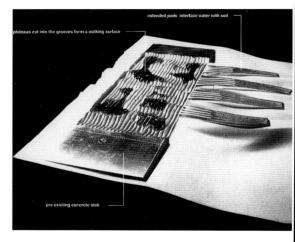

extended pads interface water with soil
plateaus cut into the grooves form a walking surface
pre-existing concrete slab

URBAN VITALITY IN MODULAR PLANES
Parque del Torrent Ballester
Barcelona, Spain, 1997, Arturo
Frediani Sarfati

In architect Sarfati's scheme for open public space in Barcelona, seemingly coincidental planes overlap and layer to create simple but rich civic theatre. Urban movement, individual human activities and vegetal structure are compositionally adjacent, yet quite visually distinct, like the multiplicity of the city itself. Pathways, promenades and plazas are not used to connect one pedestrian space to another, rather, the entirety of the park is a fully accessible subdivision of non-hierarchical units. Nature is not an untouched other that is framed and viewed from a given point, but is instead an equal module alongside built elements. Programming is largely left to the users. Sarfati values the 'vitality of human beings' by allowing park visitors to make their own pathways over time, and expects the landscape to 'develop a unity according to its own laws'. The angled planes of pavement, water and plantings evolve, slowly changing their experiential identity and dimensions over time in response to neighbourhood needs.

Order and

Objects

Nature is an ordered system, and the wise designer heeds its advice.

Creation and destruction are antithetical notions in human terms,
but they are synonymous for the gods.   **Octavio Paz**[1]

Farmer, scientist, artist, poet: no matter the pursuit, order leads to efficiency. In the creation of gardens, order promotes understanding. An ordering system, be it organic or applied, facilitates function and insinuates form (which the designer may or may not choose to develop within the site). In the realm of the radical, order may be unrecognizable at first, particularly if it involves a purposeful departure from the known. Yet the logic exists, and is worth looking for.

Philosophers have claimed that since the time of the Renaissance, Western artists have been caught in the mystical web of space and in the pursuit of new ways to see the things that surround them. In the practice of landscape architecture and garden design, the means to measure and to quantify – to see – form and spatial volume (and their corollaries, proportion and scale) is constantly sought. Although many factors come into play, it is the arrangement of objects within a site that defines spatial relationships and manifest order. The coming together of object and space is the unification of opposites, as inseparable as Paz's acts of creation and destruction.

The first step, therefore, in understanding new landscapes is to investigate their ordering technique, a task best approached by evaluating the placement of objects in relation to the surrounding context, or the composition of parts within the whole. Noting that 'order without diversity can result in monotony or boredom; diversity without order can produce chaos',[2] the designers in this book employ innovative formal arrangements, but do not abandon legibility or structural clarity. While several projects in this chapter are examples of outstanding contemporary site organization, others represent object studies that explore the more intimate co-dependency of form and space.

Peter Walker has long been recognized for his strength of design orders and powerful site geometries. Walker appreciates that objects mark the land and create spatial tension, and that such ordering principles as symmetry, hierarchy, seriality and patterning have the ability to simplify and to abstract. At IBM Makuhari (p. 58), Walker designed an 'abstract, modern, geometric composition'[3] intended to be viewed from offices above as much as to be experienced from within. In this sense – the duality of the experiential framework – the project is an apt reference to the multiplicity of modes of communication in contemporary society.

As a series of contemplative courtyards, the IBM Makuhari garden is overtly unified by the placement of objects within outdoor rooms. Although the materials and their use vary across the site, the structural pattern is consistent and so easily perceived that visitors are left with no ambiguity. Families of objects read as integral spatial units – the benches and sun screens on the sky terrace, the evergreen hedge segments that ground the Sentinel Stone, or the bamboo groves that bracket the linear site. In contrast, single objects punctuate the overriding order with poignant statements of individuality. Consistency and interruption are two sides of the same coin: establishment of visual and physical destinations. The garden's highly ordered layout, initially inspired by the image of an early computer punch card, attempts to raise the 'theme of tension among nature, art, and technology', reflecting 'a current in the vanguard of contemporary installation art, expressing a cultural idea of discord among the three disciplines'.[4]

At the other end of the spectrum, Jesús Moroles's Spirit Fountains (p. 66) represent the pure creation of energized space. Whereas IBM Makuhari fulfils a courtyard layout enclosed by buildings, the serpentine granite columns of Spirit Fountains stand alone. Moroles's interest in the ingredients of spatial volumetrics is expressed in this project, where he plays with the delicate dynamics of formal nuance. Moroles is trying to create spaces as opposed to objects at this stage in his career. Yet can the two be separated? Just when does the void between objects become a palpable force? In this project, order is more intuitive than graphic, and you have the sense that there is no enforced border or edge to the site. Rather, the Spirit Fountains draw visitors in, and due to their open-ended spatial flow – an activation of an area rather than a compartmentalization – they may even follow visitors as they walk away.

Taking a different tack in the exploration of order and object, the gorgeous estate of Mas de les Voltes (p. 72) by Fernando Caruncho at first appears quite traditional in its composition. Upon closer inspection, however, it becomes evident that historic agricultural prototypes have been altered and abstracted. Endless wheat fields have become concise parterres. The linear element that reinforces the processional central axis – alternating cypress and fruit trees – are extracts from the archetypal wind rows and orchard. Placid reflecting pools are direct descendants of the cistern. Gnarled vines, typically seen in tended vineyards of industrial dimensions, are reinterpreted here as decorative plantings on the architecturally cut slope that mediates between the domestic terrace and the lower garden. A sense of serene order and organization pervades the grounds; perhaps derived in equal part from the farm plots' mathematical precision and the pleasure found in basic geometries of complementary proportions.

In a similar manner, the grounds at the Esso Headquarters (p. 76) by Kathryn Gustafson, lend a twist on the landscape tradition. Gustafson sees value in the exclusive corporate greensward, and bases her design concept on a careful assessment of the relationship between building and site. Shadows cast by the edifice on the solstice and equinox dictate curves in the garden plan, while narrow runnels transect the willow-dotted lawn and connect the corporate body to the Seine River. In the scheme, segments are never intended to stand alone; the very nature and Nature of the site indicate an overarching sublimation of individual tendencies to a greater whole. The pastoral model is acknowledged as a precedent, but clearly balanced structure prevails over imitation of Nature.

Which comes first in the creation of contemporary landscapes, form or space? The exact design genesis surely differs from designer to designer, from site to site and in consideration of land use. It may be that for most designers there is a simultaneous recognition of system and content. As Bachelard posited, 'the coexistence of things in a space to which we add consciousness of our own existence, is a very concrete thing'.[5]

1 Interview with Octavio Paz. Artes de Mexico (no. 9, Autumn 1990): 99.
2 Ching, Francis. Architecture: Form, Space & Order (New York: Van Nostrand Reinhold, 1979): 332.
3 Walker, Peter and Leah Levy. Peter Walker: Minimalist Gardens (Washington, DC: Spacemaker Press, 1997): 143.
4 Ibid.
5 Bachelard, Gaston. The Poetics of Space (New York: Orion Press, 1964).

METAPHOR IN THE GARDEN
IBM Makuhari
Chiba Prefecture, Japan, 1991, Peter Walker and Partners

Landscape and garden design is very much a means of communication. At IBM Makuhari, a series of contemplative courtyards could be interpreted as the landscape equivalent of a computer punch card in the sense that pattern reveals information and, in Leah Levy's words, as 'a metaphor for ordering the infinite possibilities in both technology and nature' (Walker, Peter and Leah Levy. Peter Walker: Minimalist Gardens. Washington, DC: Spacemaker Press, 1997).

In the courtyard garden, surrounded by the corporate building envelope, the relationship between architecture and garden is multifaceted: the green spaces can be alternatively (or simultaneously) understood as a foreground to the built backdrop – unified with the vertical glass surfaces by reflection – or as an inner sanctum of the building. Because the courtyard scheme is intensely ordered, it easily reads as an extension of, or a nesting within, the architecture. However, the gardens are inherently a very intimate juxtaposition of 'other' against Taniguchi and Associates' eleven-storey slate-clad structure. Implicit in the serial ordering of the space are equal gestures to technological efficiency and meditative purity. →

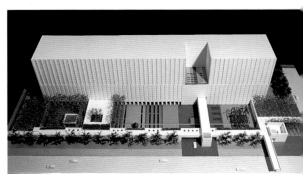

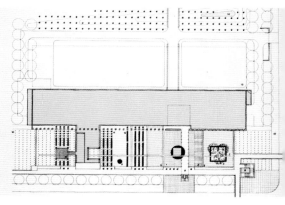

→ Primary function areas (gallery, lobby, café, conference rooms) overlook the highly controlled composition of stone, water and plant material. Recalling aspects of traditional Japanese gardens, each ingredient is selected and cared for with a level of detail that is both poetic and ascetic. Plaited sub-spaces are created by repeated clipped hedges, low stone walls, gridded bamboo stalks and pools of water. Crisply detailed paving and plantings bring the scale of the ordering strategy to a minute level to the degree that 'the distinction between organic matter and mineral elements is blurred'. From the density of the water lilies' floating foliage to the jade pebbles' shade of green, serendipity does not play a significant role here.

The practice avoids sterile geometries. At IBM Makuhari, the flow of ordered volumes is heightened and punctuated by focus objects (such as the Sentinel Stone, above) and by an awareness of light. By day, sunlight glitters on the pools or is filtered by bamboo, willows and screens. One's perception of depth is teased by reflective glass surfaces. At night, a glowing line traverses most of the garden, linking the outdoor spaces to each other and to the enveloping architecture.

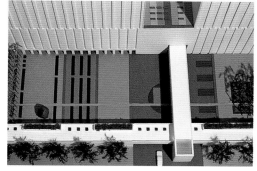

The arrangement of
objects within a site
defines spatial
relationships and
manifest order.

ACHIEVING PERSPECTIVE
Garden for VSB
Utrecht, The Netherlands, 1995, West 8
Landscape Architects

In considering the power or success of a particular ordering scheme, scale is paramount. In West 8's corporate garden for the VSB headquarters, scale is a shifting quality left to the viewer's discretion. At its most grand, one sees the garden as an object itself: a circumscribed, textured 656-foot (200 metres) rectangle stapled to the earth by a free-form bridge structure, juxtaposed against the sleek, 295-foot-high (90 metres) mass of the office block. Stepping closer, the garden becomes an organization of holly-hedge segments interspersed with five red sandstone cairns and transected by a bridge. Entering the sunken space, the detailed planting plan and the individual elements that make up the fragmented, linear order of the garden's interior are apparent. According to the designers, the multiplicity of readings puts the composite elements 'into some sort of perspective', but does not require adherence to any one interpretation.

At the time of the headquarter's construction, protests from supporters of the adjacent Bloeiendael Ecological Park made it clear that the high-rise must have a mediating landscape. The design team created a raised planted plinth to accommodate below-grade parking and installed a grove of birches to ground the building's height. The nearby sunken labyrinth of clipped hedge segments set on a plane of red gravel acts as a sculpture garden of sorts for the corporate workforce.

The reptilian-style steel bridge extends a pedestrian route from the bordering ecological park through the corporate grounds.

[above bottom] **THE OBJECT OF SPACE**
Spirit Fountains
Changchun, China, 1999, Jesús Moroles
Artist and stonemason Jesús Moroles says that he is 'trying to
create spaces at this point in my life'. It is clear that his latest
efforts achieve a more nuanced resonant dialogue between form
and space than his earlier work. In the park's entry plaza, eleven
figures carved from granite stand in a 40-foot-diameter (12 metres)
circle. The curvaceous objects, although freestanding, are perceived
as an energized whole. Moroles shaped stone, but it was space that
he was creating.

[left and above top] **INCIDENTS ALONG THE WAY**
Birmingham Botanical Garden
Alabama, US, 1998, Jesús Moroles
As visitors get out of their cars and move toward the Botanical
Garden they encounter Moroles's bollard sculpture. Farther in,
a 'granite garden' of spiralled columns (the precursor to Spirit
Fountains) draws the curious.

TRADITION AND INVENTION
Les Confines
St-Rémy-de-Provence, France, 1993, Dominique Lafourcade
Traditional axial ordering techniques are adhered to by regularly spaced hedge segments, cypress trees and potted olives in this contemporary French garden. The irrigation channel is emphasized by a collar of lamb's ear. Lafourcade sees the line of water as the garden's spine, both a nourishing lifeline and a primary element of site structure.

REFLECTING ON PATTERN
NTT Musashino R+D Center
Tokyo, Japan, 1999, Yoji Sasaki

For national communications giant NTT, landscape architect Yoji Sasaki sought to incorporate 'the visual, sensual, and symbolic idea of reflection' into a corporate garden that doubles as an urban pocket park. Tension is subliminally present in the interplay of identical chequerboard squares of water and turf (see pp. 54–55), a design that perhaps stems from Sasaki's delineation between public and private space.

Cherry trees rising off the gridded forecourt of the R+D Center are reflected in the building's glass face and in the pools. The iconic species connects the corporate garden to its city surrounds by linking to an existing cherry-lined promenade. In response to NTT's requirement for tight security, the site is bordered by planted mounds (Sasaki chose to avoid high walls that would visually cut the garden off from the street). The alternating panels of water prevent visitors from approaching other than along the approved pathways that connect the private edifice to the public realm – a very functional use of water that produces a powerful aesthetic of ordered terrain.

Such ordering principles
as symmetry, seriality and
patterning have the ability
to simplify and to abstract.

PULLING CONTEXT INTO SITE TEXT
Osawano Kenko Fureai Park
Toyama, Japan, 1999, Hiroki Hasegawa/Studio on Site

Landscape architect Hiroki Hasegawa and colleagues
began by reading land-use patterns in the area
surrounding the site. A patchwork of orthogonal sectors
defined by intersecting paths and water trenches
heightens the connection to the agricultural context
and, in Hasegawa's words, 'makes a garden without
boundary'. The park's flexible, modular composition
aids its phased implementation. The site model illustrates
how programme elements and areas of play fit within the
overall site structure of the 13.6-acre (5.5 hectares)
community park.

CULTIVATING CLARITY
Mas de les Voltes
Spain, 1994, Fernando Caruncho

A classicist at first glance, landscape architect Fernando Caruncho takes traditional crops, harvest techniques and water-collection methods and rearranges them to find a modernist spatial sensibility. At Caruncho's agricultural estate, pure planes and individual objects establish orientations that extend far beyond the given site and time. Distilled to their most basic geometry, orchards, vineyards, wheat fields and cisterns form a composition where ontology and oenology coexist.

For structural and visual strength the pool is subdivided into four sections. Mowed grass aisles divide the four-square of water and extend view corridors beyond the property lines. Cultivated textures bring to life readily legible hierarchies: the gnarled stance of olive trees alongside columnar cypress, tiers of twisted grapevines descending toward placid mirrors of water, bristled masses of golden wheat stalks framed by velvet-smooth clipped turf. With moves that echo the ancients, Mas de les Voltes blurs the distinction between domestic space and productive grounds.

In the creation of gardens, order promotes understanding.

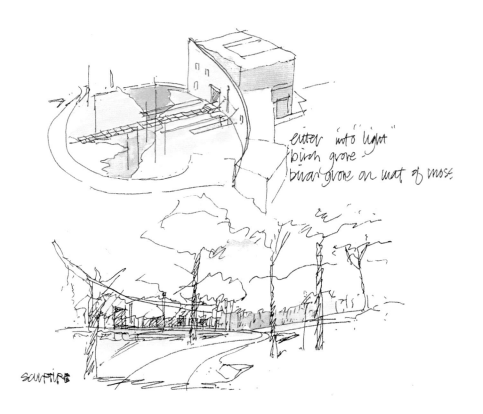

enter into light
birch grove
birch grove on mat of moss

sculpture

[left and opposite] **A THRESHOLD FORGED BETWEEN
FOREST AND ARCHITECTURE**
Private Residence
Vermont, US, 1998, The Office of H. Keith Wagner

Landscape architect, painter, sculpture, metalsmith:
H. Keith Wagner explores his inspiration in numerous
media. Examined in model, oil paints, sketches,
photographs and a haiku by Japanese poet Basho,
the project's design parti is founded on an 'abstracted
representation of the architecture and the site
expressed in a simple, bold gesture .... Geometry and
rhythm derive their cadence from the architectural
datum and the site's axial forces both locally and
regionally.' Wagner's sketches consider the relationship
between architecture and courtyard, and depict the
approach as visitors pass through the native forest
and 'enter into light' (see pp. 28–29).

The sweeping stone arc of the house façade
is echoed by a low wall of local Panton stone that
separates the drop-off area from the inner band
of courtyard. While the mixed forest encompasses
the curved segment of wall on the arrival side, on
the other side of the wall is an uncluttered swath
of mounded moss. This confirms that architecture
and nature, while complementary in this scenario,
are two distinct entities with a threshold of energized
space between them.

[below] **FORCES OF INSIGHT**
Bicentennial Hall
**Middlebury College, Vermont, US, 1999, The Office
of H. Keith Wagner**

A collage by Wagner investigates the site forces that
give compositional order to a new campus landscape.

The multifaceted approach to site design was a cornerstone of Wagner's creative process in the development of the mountainside residential landscape.

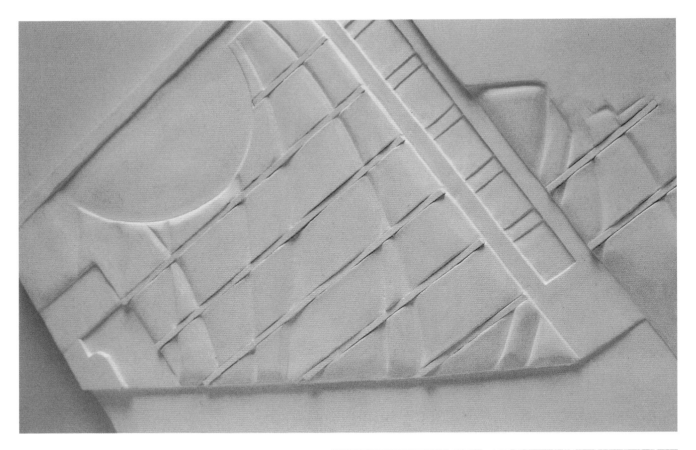

SUBTLE STEPS TO URBANITY
Esso Headquarters
Rueil-Malmaison, France, 1992, Kathryn Gustafson

'I work with the ground. From the contact with the ground I try to evoke emotions,' explains landscape architect Kathryn Gustafson. At the Esso Headquarters near Paris – designed by architects Viguier and Jodry – the ground is sectioned by narrow water channels and has a pastoral sprinkling of willow trees. The 3.2-acre (1.3 hectares) scheme unites the new architecture with an established site alongside the Seine River to, as Gustafson puts it, 'research a new urbanity that respects the existing scale and richness of the environment'.

Shadows cast by the new building became the compositional lines of the garden. Gustafson calculated the exact orientation of sunlight and shade on the solstice and the equinox and incorporated the result into the plan. A long pool bordered by shallow steps and a ramp mark the main entrance and link the headquarters directly to the river. The pool is fed by the series of canals that transect the site and herald changes in grade as the garden slopes from contemporary built form to the historic Seine.

Revealing Interaction

Sometimes it takes a designer's subtle hand to make visible the most basic and meaningful aspects of our complex environment.

Subject both of science and art, the landscape functions as a mirror and a lens:
in it we see the space we occupy and ourselves as we occupy it.
Jeffrey Kastner and Brian Wallis[1]

Possibly the most intriguing and most confounding aspect of landscape design is the phenomenon of continual change. Change in seasons, daily cycles, weather, movement of water and wind, processes of growth, degeneration and chemical exchange and the effects of human behaviour over time all coincide to shape the evolution of any given place. While we can predict and accommodate the majority of these conditions, certain influences are difficult to manage or even to discover. Some of the most exciting contemporary landscape design accesses the unseen or disguised actions within the environment, interceding in previously invisible processes as a generator of design concept.

Unlike many recent projects that insinuate design structure into an existing or revitalized ecosystem, the projects shown in this chapter are more about producing mechanisms that reveal rather than systems that interpret. The work here tends to focus on one or two discrete environmental phenomena, and is conceived of as a tool for bringing forth those effects – not as an act of integration or assimilation, but as an act of signification as the idiosyncrasies of place and time combine with designed landscape elements to create a third entity. Neither is the dominant ingredient. Both garden mechanism and climatic/temporal ephemera are required to set the scheme in motion. It is the interaction of the two bodies – one incarnate, one without tangible substance – that expose the poetics of the unseen forces that shape our world.

For example, Makoto Sei Watanabe's Fiber Wave (p. 102) consists of, in the material sense, a collection of thin carbon-fibre poles. The 14.8-foot-high (4.5 metres) poles stand still in the calm air and are illuminated by solar chips. The scheme is not enacted until the wind blows and the flexible light rods begin to sway, giving substance and tactility to invisible air currents. Watanabe calls it 'learning from Nature', and refers to the lithe character of organisms that 'assume the posture which requires the least expenditure of energy'. Casting light from the tip of the wind rods, the solar-powered diodes exhibit a replenishable interplay between man's technology and nature's resources by feeding on natural energy to induce a designed environment.

While not random, the project's outcome is not predictable. Watanabe's 'design-less design' sets up a structure, but does not attempt to define expected results. A 'code' of responsive characteristics is put in place, but the true outcome relies on fickle components. Watanabe's work is attuned to dynamic forces of nature, such as wind direction, wind strength and solar exposure. However, as with Studio on Site's roof garden at the YKK R&D Center (p. 92), no one enforces those rules – both practices set the stage and step away. As Studio on Site points out, 'each thing inserted into the landscape ... acts as a catalyst'.

The Dew Gardens by Chris Parsons (p. 82) expose an interaction so commonplace that we rarely take notice of its occurrence. It is Homer's 'daughter of the dawn'[2] – the early morning hours and the condensation of dew – that Parsons uses to etch an ephemeral image into the close-clipped turf of a bowling green. An interesting aspect of the gardens is that the genius loci comes not from a specific place, but rather, from a precise time. Dew forms between dusk and dawn and the drops only survive the first three hours or so of light. In a way, each garden experience is anchored in the fourth dimension – time – rather than in a mappable site. In fact, Parsons hopes to replicate the process in a number of other locales. The only essentials are time of day, the presence of humidity and someone to sweep the grass.

The landscape architect must be as careful when designing in time as when designing in space. Sense of spatial scale has a dramatic effect on the perception of the designed landscape – the same is true when working with the medium of time. If you look at the Dew Gardens on a daily basis, the sweeping at dawn determines the pattern of light and colour and literally brings the gardens into existence again and again – a nearly miraculous, continuous rebirth that symbolizes the living, growing, cyclical art of gardens on a very condensed time line. If you consider the gardens in a more existentialist context, i.e., that they are present only after sweeping the dew and cease to exist once the dew drops have evaporated and no pattern is visible, then the time frame is reduced to several hours, after which the gardens become icons of regression and loss. They truly are works that man puts into play and then allows nature to take its course.

The role of the designer/implementer is notably different in the various landscapes presented in this chapter. There is the 'divine being', who sets a project in motion and then leaves the landscape to its own devices; but there is also the 'micro manager', for whom the human hand is one of the crucial cogs in the design process. The majority of projects shown here fall somewhere between the two, operating more along the lines of the former. However, the latter is provocative due to its underlying assumption that the designer is subordinate to the end result. The idea that the designed landscape does not exist unless occupied by or enlivened by a person allows us a degree of power over our environment, yet simultaneously values our role as just another species on the stage of landscapes in flux.

There is a meditative element to be appreciated in contemporary work that is derived from the numerous and subtle interactions that compose our environment. Reductive human action – discovering rather than adding – carried out with the most basic tools can be extremely powerful. In these cases, the designer constructs a garden by focusing on phenomena that already exist. For instance, it is the ability to wield a broom and devise a pattern that fuels the Dew Gardens, but it is the glistening, perishable congress of sunlight, moisture and clipped turf that is the work.

Projects of interactive revelation tend to raise the question: just what are the parameters of a garden and, specifically in the Dew Gardens, where, if anywhere, is the fine line between performance, installation and garden design? Perhaps it is best to permit ambiguity to breed richness of interpretation. For instance, the Dew Gardens cannot be occupied at will because they exist for just a brief moment each day. They require a ridiculous ratio of handiwork to finished product (a ratio that would never stand up to the efficiency litmus tests of mass commodification, unless photographs or other representations were considered sufficient replications of the projects). They are so very difficult to achieve and cannot be purchased – is that why we value things of beautiful happenstance, delicacy and momentariness?

The garden at Yoji Sasaki's White Rain House (p. 98) acts as a theatre of interaction between climatic activity and the materials that make up personal space. This common space – in which the intimate choice of style and cultural proclivities are displayed – varies significantly from home to home, between private and public areas, from region to region. What is revealed? Moods, emotions, habits, a lifetime of experiences, all played out in the forms, structure, layout and programming of a landscape. If I choose to pave my courtyard with asphalt and you densely plant yours with layers of shrubbery and ground cover, our worlds will be very different when it rains. And, when there is no choice: if I grow up on the streets, where a strong, swirling wind coats everything with sand and grit, while you love the winds because they cause apples to drop onto a grassy field for easy harvesting, we will each seek environments that protect or expose us to breezes based on these experiences. The force at work, the natural phenomenon exposed through interaction, is the human psyche. This begins, as Makoto Sei Watanabe writes in his project statement, 'when people see and respond to what they see with empathy. That is the mission of architecture and the role of art, as well.'

1 Kastner, Jeffrey and Brian Wallis. Land and Environmental Art (London: Phaidon Press, 1998): 11.
2 Webster's New World College Dictionary (fourth edition).

THE TRANSITORY NATURE OF ART
Dew Gardens
Various locations, 1998–, Chris Parsons

Now you see it, now you don't. One dawn, while sweeping a bowling green, artist Chris Parsons, at that time employed as a park groundsman, had an epiphany. Struck by the vivid contrast between the clean-swept turf and the still dewy surfaces, Parsons found a new medium and a new canvas. What does a dew artist do? Most importantly, beat the sun. To be successful, a design must be etched in the dew-heavy grass before the sun's heat causes the strokes to transpire into thin air.

Ephemerality does not erase the potency of Parsons's pictures. Photography is a crucial aspect of his work – each garden is captured on film before evaporating. The artist spends up to several hours implementing his designs, while the finished product exists for less than four hours depending on the day's weather. Moving from simple geometric patterns to more complex 1960s-style op art graphics, Parsons continues to develop his work and has carried out guest installations – or performance pieces – abroad.

There is a meditative element to be appreciated in contemporary work that is derived from the numerous and subtle interactions that compose our environment.

REWARDING CREATIVE FERTILITY
Festival International des Jardins, Chaumont-sur-Loire, France, 1996–99, various designers

Chaumont-sur-Loire's annual festival of themed garden installations revels in the idiosyncrasies of creative thought. Pictured here: [above and opposite top] **Saules dans la Brume** Designed in 1996 by Judy and David Drew of the UK, woven willows and a trellis support new leaf growth. The display thickens over time as the sun and a microclimate of mist provide nourishment. [opposite middle] **Le Baobab qui Pleure** Designed in 1997 by E. Boulmier, F. Kiene and the Conservatoire de Chaumont, France. An image derived from Africa, the ancient tree 'cries' with its blossoming branches. [opposite bottom and middle right] **Trognes** Designed in 1997 by D. Mansion, France, the traditional agricultural practice of tree-topping is appreciated as a living sculpture. [top right] **Gaspatio Andaluz** Designed in 1999 by Agence in Situ, France. Recovered olive-oil drums serve as planters for the ingredients of a well-known Andalusian cold soup. [right, second from top] **Potager Nomade** Designed in 1999 by P. Nadeau, V. Dupont-Rougier and J. Alexandre, France. A contemporary fold-up garden with greenhouse, terrace and portable furrows. [right, bottom and second from bottom] **Nebelgarten** Designed in 1999 by P. Latz and Associates, Germany. Bavarian stones trimmed into a spiral plan cut angled windows for curious visitors, while mists encourage vine growth and play with the light.

A 'dramatic point of contact with the surrounding landscape'

DAILY CYCLES ON STAGE
Naganuma Community Park
Hokkaido, Japan, 1992, Yoji Sasaki
The project brochure reads 'Nature's Drama – Water Theater'. Although it is intended to host human performances and recreation, the stark structuring of the park's open-air theatre draws attention to a natural drama: the everyday interactions of water, light and reflection. They are commonplace happenings, but are rarely noticed or celebrated. In form and in use, the Water Theater spotlights the sun's sequence.

Described by the design team as a 'dramatic point of contact with the surrounding landscape', the Water Stage reaches into a wide pool at the foot of amphitheatre seating. Open-ended forms – archetypal, but without restricting identity – allow the interplay of water, light and solid form to take centre stage.

REVELATION IN TIME OF PLACE
Après la Grande Tempête – Trois Cheminées de Desmarest
L'Usine Ephémère, Centre d'Art Comtemporain,
Desmarest, France, 1990, David Jones

A connection between the natural forest and industrial
production, the work of artist David Jones strives 'to make
sense of the earth involving the elements of air, earth, fire,
and water'. Fabricated as part of a major exhibition at the
defunct Desmarest button factory (now a contemporary art
space), the work was created from a multi-trunked chestnut
tree that fell during the violent storms of 1989. In half of
the project, Jones made three chimneys from the trunks,
each approximately 13 feet (4 metres) high, corresponding
to the factory's remaining three chimneys. The trunks were
split and hollowed, filled with dry wood, resealed with clay
from under the roots of the original tree, and fired to enact
the performance aspect of the project. Jones considered
the silence of the old factory machinery as a metaphor for
the calm after the intensity of the Industrial Revolution,
relating the natural phenomena of the tempest to the
destructive forces of industrial production. Inside
the factory, Jones filled a series of boat forms (made
from the branches of the chestnut tree) with buttons
and shell remnants found on site. The Trochus shells
came, coincidentally, from the artist's homeland over
one hundred years ago.

[pp. 90–91] **AREAS OF INFLUENCE**
Various sites, David Jones

David Jones engages the landscape using the primary human senses, attempting to understand something of the ritual associated with the intersection of place and natural phenomena. In signifying seemingly insignificant things, places, objects or sensations, he brings forth personal interpretations of the natural world, pulling invisibilities into our sphere of perception. Photographic documentation is essential in Jones's artistic process. The 'Areas of Influence' pictured here are studies of very specific features of the land, but also of the space between spaces that seems not to be important. 'I see an affinity with the Australian Aboriginal people, who have no word for "artist" or "art". They see the activity which Western culture identifies as "art" as being a means by which they can make sense of the environment, time and place,' says Jones.

[top row, p. 90] **Mardarburdar Alignment II, 1989**
In summer, the dry lake's salty crust is pure white, underlaid with red iron oxide. The elements cut by Jones (and later cast in iron) and the purposeful human presence creates an alignment with nearby Mardarburdar Hill. The artist's figure is covered with pigment from beneath the lake's surface.

[middle row, p. 90] **Perspective I and Perspective II, 1976**
At dry Lake Austin, Jones works with the shimmering mirage of the horizon. It is a bodily engagement with the place, a kind of sensing and describing as the lake's surface is scribed in a 98-foot-long (30 metres) spiral walkway to reveal red iron oxide beneath the veneer of white salt.

[bottom row, p. 90] **Lieu Vert aux Fourmis Rouges, 1988**
At the centre for contemporary art in Limousin, France, Jones and other artists created 'sculpture as place'. Exploring materials as cultural descriptors, he installed an 82-foot-long (25 metres) iron serpentine form, cast from trees that had fallen into Lake Vasivière. 'It is like a fossil, the memory of form pressed into sand,' says Jones. 'It has an ominous, subtle presence; you realize only slowly that it is a man-made object.' The perfectly horizontal line comes out and re-enters the ground without beginning or end. Red ants that built a nest at one end of the line are an integral aspect of the design.

[top row, p. 91] **Kunturu (Kuntrin), Australian Aboriginal Stone Placement, 1976–93**
A source of epiphany documented by Jones over nearly twenty years, the remote stone spiral is estimated to be three hundred years old. Is it a way-marker, a water locater, a symbol of ritual? 'It is more than an aesthetic experience of a physical object,' says Jones. 'In Carl Andre's words, "in places like this, there is a kind of calm, a fierce calm … a fierce equilibrium".'

[middle row, p. 91] **Fuji Alignment – Homage to Mardarburdar, 1990**
Near Yokohama, flaming sky reflects onto the wet, black sand, appearing like fire along the shoreline. Sand excavated from a narrow trench is tipped into a positive form. Suddenly Mount Fuji appears, echoing the constructed mound. 'What is Mardarburdar?' asks Jones, 'Like a grain of sand on this beach is to Mount Fuji – nothing! Nowhere! But they depend on each other.'

[bottom row, p. 91] **Earth Form, 1979**
Referencing the Australian landscape that is scarred and sculpted by fire and water, Jones installed two forms made from Jarrah, an indigenous red hardwood. Fire shapes the pieces; its progression halted by water just before the exhibit opens. Plumes of steam indicate the presence of the work.

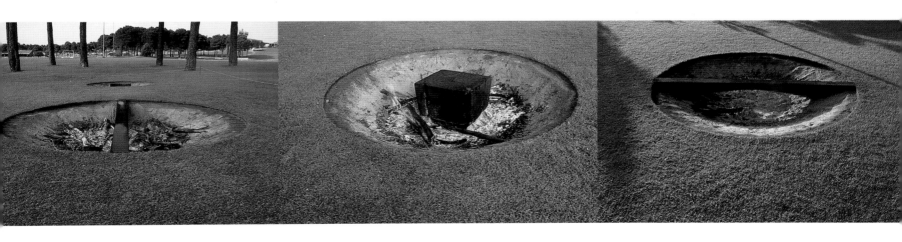

PHENOMENA DISTILLED FOR THE EYE TO SEE
YKK R+D Center Roof Garden
Tokyo, Japan, 1993, Toru Mitani/Studio on Site

The physical parameters of the YKK rooftop courtyard
are defined by office space, an exhibition hall, a café and
a hotel. Designer Toru Mitani's intent was to create a self-
contained situation, flexible enough to have long-term
effectiveness. Opting for abstract forms over symbolic
portrayal (the more traditional approach in Japanese
gardens), Mitani believes that 'any representative story
would soon be boring for the office workers' who look
down at the garden day after day.

Therefore, the elements of the nearly 7,000-square-
foot (650 square metres) courtyard are structurally
well-defined and graphically evocative, but their
primary gestalt is a coordinated response to the natural
phenomena of weather and sunlight. 'The geometry
for the scheme is absolutely simple' and not intended
'to impress its own existence', says Mitani. Rather,
'this garden is designed to exist here just like a mirror
of the environment.'

At the heart of the roof garden, a circle of black
granite is misted by a grid of water jets. When glistening
with moisture, the granite appears as 'a mirror against
the sky', reflecting the passage of clouds and daylight.
The black circle also takes on a sense of depth when
viewed from above. Rising like a curtain pulled tightly
around the circle's edge, a ring of bamboo catches
the breeze as wind is channelled between the closely
spaced buildings. Office workers looking out can gauge
the weather by observing the garden.

According to the design team, highly customized
paving details are interactive. As people move through
the complex around the courtyard they see different
colour schemes. Patterned steel grating and modular
stone pavers set in a harlequin chequerboard seem
to shift depending on the viewpoint, an optical play
on the horizontal plane that animates the space to
a remarkable degree.

The client requested that a steel sculpture be installed
outside the president's quarters. Choosing to avoid
a single focal object, Mitani and associates developed
a matrix of forty-four 'wind fish' as a multipart dynamic
weather vane. The fish 'swim' in the urban wind currents
that would otherwise swirl by the windows unseen.

Details of the wind fish, and a view of the roof garden as seen from the offices above.

DETAILS BROUGHT FORTH TO PROVOKE AND INSPIRE
Atlantis-Mariposa Think Tank
Tenerife, Canary Islands, 1993–, Helga and Hans-Jürgen Müller
(promoters and directors)

The majority of revelational designs shown in this chapter focus on forces of the natural environment. At the Mariposa garden, site features are personal interpretations of the creators' interaction with different kinds of energy: local culture and regional attitudes toward the role of nature in place-making. The project is realized over time by more than fifty international artists, each of whom selects an aspect, an eco-cultural process or a particular spot of the property with which to work. No time limits are set for the fruition of an idea. Inspiration is cultivated on the site, and design development also occurs there: the typical methods of drawing, modelling and computer representation are not used.

The site occupies an exposed rocky slope with south-western orientation. Art, architecture and landscape coexist as one expression of cultural probing. The garden is a net of episodes and events. A catalogue of the project begins with Leonardo da Vinci's thought, 'Knowledge not perceived through the senses can produce no other than a harmful truth'. The Mariposa Think Tank has a clear ideological, even prophetic purpose; the founders hope that the compound will serve as a workshop where visiting politicians, industrialists, scientists, artists and philosophers can brainstorm about triggering change for future generations. The project literature describes the project as an 'immediately recognizable center of aesthetic aspirations ... as a place and source of cultural being .... The beauty of place designed by artists is not only exalting in an emotional sense, but also inspires thought.'

Revealing Interaction

INTERCEDING IN EPHEMERALITIES
White Rain House
Osaka, Japan, 1999, Yoji Sasaki

'The White Rain House and landscape is responding to the ephemeral qualities of light, wind, color, and water,' explains landscape architect Yoji Sasaki. Constructed as a residential complex of one-room apartments in collaboration with architect Akira Sakamoto, the project is designed to bring sensations of nature to the forefront of the residents' daily experience. House and landscape are said to change appearance from moment to moment, undergoing visual and material adjustments that key in observers to natural phenomena. →

→ Capturing temporality and expressing mutability are implicit motivations underlying the schematics of the White Rain House courtyard. Throughout the day, assemblages of the vegetation and building materials (stone, concrete, glass) are engaged in an ever-changing interplay of colour and texture. Elements such as the delicate screen fence, rails and trees share a dialogue of light and shadow, mutually casting lines and shades of darkness that weave together on the ground plane. Rainwater accentuates certain surfaces and obscures others. Night lighting brings an entirely different cast on the characters. As a whole, the composition is a legible text, proffering information about daily and seasonal cycles. Individually, parts are read as actors on a stage; self-conscious in their graceful simplicity, silent between revealing acts.

Moods, emotions, habits, a lifetime of experiences are all played out in the forms, structure, layout and programming of a garden.

SUPPLE STRUCTURES IN STEP WITH THE WIND
K-Museum/Fiber Wave
Tokyo, Japan, 1995, Makoto Sei Watanabe

Architect Makoto Sei Watanabe has been working on the
idea of a Fiber Wave over several projects and in various
forms. The K-Museum and its grounds reveal the
infrastructure of a vast failed new sub-city, an area that
'came into being only after having destroyed the local
ecosystem'. On the empty landscape, the Fiber Wave
installation defines an energized field that breathes life
into the stillborn urban centre. One hundred and fifty thin
carbon-fibre rods, 14.7 feet (4.5 metres) high, each hold
a solar battery and a blue light-emitting diode at their tip.
The free-standing strands sway at the wind's lightest touch
and bend deeply in a strong breeze (see pp. 78–79). At night,
the diodes release the sun's energy and suggest twinkling
stars in the urban depths. The architect describes the work
as 'design-less design', as simply following nature's rules
of morphology to articulate patterns latent in the wind.

Never immobile, Watanabe's 'supple structures' change
stance in response to wind, rain, light and temperature,
always assuming the posture that requires the least
expenditure of energy. Illuminated – seen – according
to the sun's strength, activated – actualized – in reaction
to the wind's energy, Fiber Wave is a landscape, an
installation, a barometer. Its grace and intelligence lies
in its ability to reveal invisible dynamics.

A UNION OF LANDSCAPE, ARCHITECTURE AND ART
Village Terrace/Edge of Water/Touch of Wind Fiber Wave
Gifu Prefecture, Japan, 1992, Makoto Sei Watanabe

In a tiny mountain village, Watanabe hopes to draw people
to the natural elements that the locals hold most dear:
the clear river and the deep-green mountains. His device
for doing this is a steel-framed, cantilevered deck that,
with the addition of sheet-metal roof panels, becomes
a place for gatherings, performances and meetings.
'The concept,' explains Watanabe, 'was not to leave
nature as is but to draw out the beauty of the nature
further by adding small artificial objects.'

The ground leading to the deck is entitled Edge of
Water and gives the impression of a green wave. Artificial
green architecture integrates with the forms and essence
of the surrounding nature. When the deck is used as a
stage, the billowing berms serve as seating. Immediately
adjacent lies the first of Watanabe's Fiber Wave
installations, and again the movement is not mechanical,
but is 'in step with the wind'. The scheme as a whole
realizes the designer's wish for a 'union of architecture,
landscape, and art, that in combination with the
surrounding nature, forms a complete space'.

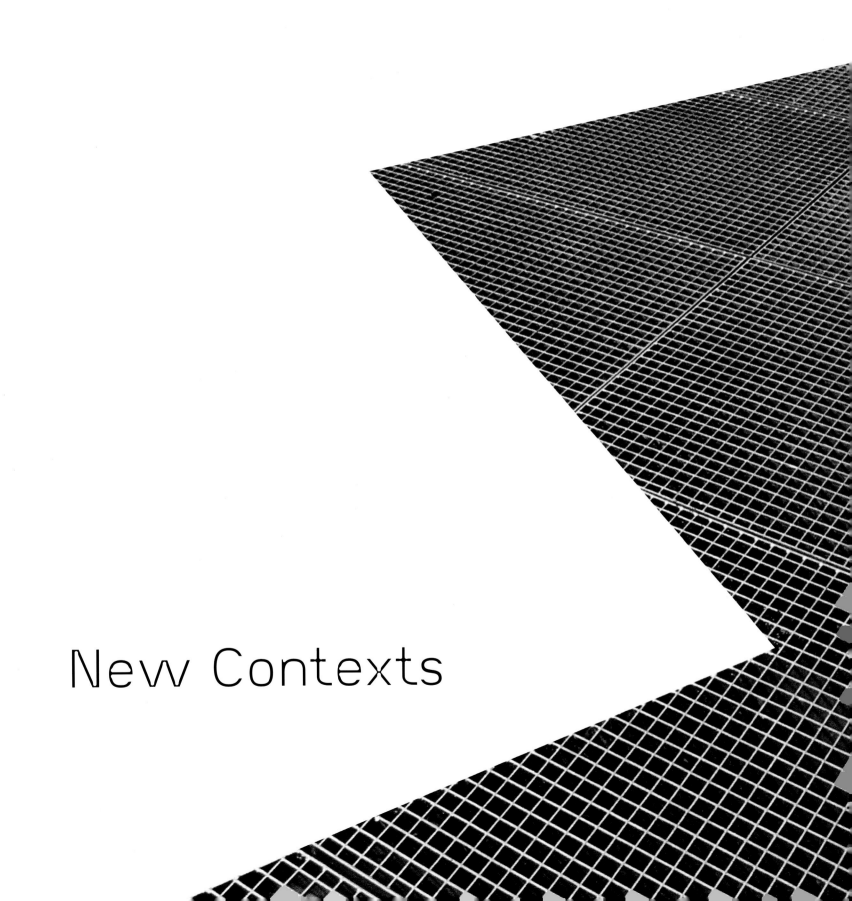

New Contexts

In today's fast-changing outdoor space, purposeful acts of landscape design are appearing in places never before considered.

> If people of different times and places have had very different ideas
> of the way a garden should be organized, it is largely because they
> have made very different assumptions, strongly affecting their aesthetic
> preferences, as to the relationship between man and nature.
>
> Elizabeth Kassler[1]

As connectivity increases exponentially and we become a networked global community, the act of place-making must retaliate. No longer is the idea of context an implication of local proximity. Materials, arrangements and forms that constitute a space may refer to and be taken from geographically, ecologically and culturally far-flung sources. The challenge, however, remains the same: the designer must create a site that is responsive to its 'text' in a meaningful way. In some cases, this results in landscapes of symbolism, such as Dani Karavan's Nursery for Peace (p. 123), that address regional themes. In other situations, a garden offers a commentary. For example, Hughes Communications entry court by Rios Associates (p. 110) playfully points to the role of technology in today's culture by incorporating a grid of satellite dishes – the heart of the client's business – as an industrial sculpture garden.

As we discuss a new contextualism, consider the semantic notion of the synecdoche: 'a figure of speech in which a part is used for a whole, an individual for a class, a material for a thing, or the reverse of any of these'[2]. In light of the complexity of today's cultural dynamics, it becomes near impossible or at best haphazard to identify, categorize and effectually react to the totality of rapidly shifting mores. Given the instability of contemporary reference points, Christopher Tunnard's question 'whither the garden?'[3] is as relevant today as when originally asked in the 1930s. Perhaps the best approach is to omit certain aspects of a site and its agenda, to simplify and to deal with a limited set of responses to context.

How to choose? Which elements, factors, strata of the encompassing environment are most crucial in forming a fitting response? Among the creators of radical landscapes, it is difficult to find common threads. Some develop inventive interpretations of programme, selecting fragments of the physical or functional fabric to weave into how people view or use a place. The appropriation of content from existing urban infrastructure or natural systems is a delicate process: done with purpose, the act reveals rich permutations; as a hollow gesture, it is soon forgotten.

Certain designers see 'non-local' mega-networks as a pertinent context and seek to establish real, virtual or symbolic connections to telecommunication, transportation and broad informational systems. These are technologically driven webs that have no real centre. They offer a very different view from our traditional understanding of the world and our place in it. They are invisible, operating outside the realm of sensory perception yet playing an essential role in our everyday lives. They are unseen geographies that govern our knowledge of things beyond the immediate place and time. In a sense, time and distance are negligible. We are as close to people on the opposite side of the globe or at the depth of the oceans or at the heights of the atmosphere, as we are to friends down the street. Spatial qualification is no longer bound by three-dimensional volume. Do we have the tools to anticipate and recognize such unfamiliar dimensions?

At present, most contemporary place-making falls short of creating radically new contextual frames. The majority of strategies focus on the nature of physical surroundings. Happily, some push past the material level and acknowledge deeper meanings and the potentially broader effects of dialogue between site, programme and context. For example, at Schiphol Airport (p. 126) the firm West 8 inserted a green haze of thousands of birch trees to infill exterior spaces. Chosen specifically for their lack of popularity with birds – the species's thin, flexible branches and catkins are not favourites with avian travellers – the trees pose an interesting link between the tradition of green parkland and the realities of airports (parking, circulation, mass influx and exodus, extreme noise and a high percentage of restricted access areas against public spaces). A project description states that 'the green haze will put into perspective the façades and viaducts and will bind together all parts of the complex – in imagery and in atmosphere – into a coherent enclave at the south axis of Amsterdam.' (Additional green cores will be incorporated along the Schiphol ring road and will eventually form a living infrastructure associated with transportation nodes around the Dutch megatropolis.) Within the airport's simple masterplan, West 8 devised several 'gardens' for plane spotters and car parking. A large void at the entrance to the airport's arrival and departure hall 'offers travellers orientation, sunlight, and fresh air'. Is it ironic that emptiness is offered to the disoriented traveller, or is it elimination of stimulation that revives us?

Kisho Kurokawa employs a very different approach at the Kuala Lumpur International Airport + Eco-Media City (p. 116), where a fragment of the native tropical rainforest is patched into the heart of the main Satellite Building. A breathing organism surrounded by glass will with time be seen from every concourse, from banks of telephones and computer hook-ups, from check-in gates and from electronic billboards. In the architect's vision, 'the symbiosis of high-tech construction details and Malaysia's rainforest brings to fruition the design concept'. One need only contemplate the facility's official title to realize the growing complexity of our changing contexts.

Dani Karavan's 1999 installation in the Piazza del Duomo in Pistoia presents a curiously disembodied garden experience. Set upon a wooden platform at the square's centre, the geometrically sectored, severely defined landscape vignette appears to hover over the piazza's ancient stone pavement. Karavan's scheme is a personal story, a memory of his father's impromptu tree nursery in the atrium of his childhood home. It is also a celebration of the city's nursery tradition and a call to peace among fractious parties and unsettled nations. In spirit, therefore, the Nursery for Peace represents multiple concentric contexts: the personal, the regional and the international. By framing and floating the garden in a modular manner, Karavan implies a fragment of text. In terms of content, it mediates between local biologies (heeled-in trees and plant materials are native, produced and sold in nearby greenhouses) and global sociologies (the idea of putting anger aside and striving together for peace). It contrasts today's suprastructures (the highways that allow us to zip out of the city into the country for a taste of nature) with historic infrastructure (an atypical planting in the heart of the traditionally open cathedral piazza). Described in the project literature as 'a work of rigorous and harmonious formal conception', the project is said to 'pose questions about humanity's fate, highlighting the value and importance of art as an element of union'.

Makoto Sei Watanabe's Jellyfish (p. 114) is a landscape of mixed parts: part house, part tool of measurement. It is 'a dwelling situated at the point where sea and land and sky come together'. One end is a translucent, invisibly contained volume of water, the other portion is a moulded piece of sky. The two exist in balance, moving up and down as solar radiation affects the weight and density of each part. In Watanabe's words, 'light is the mediator', and 'only in water can we truly grasp the three-dimensionality of space'. The context is far older than humanity, yet is rarely occupied: the fleeting and fluid threshold of atmospheric change. Much like his Fiber Wave projects (p. 102), with Jellyfish Watanabe makes intangible forces tangible.

One is hard-pressed to draw a common conclusion from the variety of projects presented in this chapter. Evidence, maybe, that culture is in a state of flux worldwide. On the verge of globalization, one wonders where the town green will feature in the global village. As with food, fashion, art, music, language and technology, traditional landscape typologies are in the process of, or soon will undergo, radical change as international influences permeate. Unlike many other entities, however, landscapes must adhere to such local conditions as light, water and climate. Or perhaps not. Above all else, a garden text has meaning only in relation to other, changing texts; the sole pretext is ambitious interpretation.

1 Kassler, Elizabeth. Modern Gardens and the Landscape (New York: Museum of Modern Art, 1964).
2 Webster's New World College Dictionary (fourth edition).
3 Tunnard, Christopher. Gardens in the Modern Landscape (London: The Architectural Press, 1938).

New Contexts

Certain designers see 'non-local' mega-networks as a pertinent context and seek to establish real, virtual or symbolic connections to telecommunications, transportation and broad informational systems.

INDUSTRIAL SCULPTURE MAKES THE SCENE
Hughes Communications Headquarters
Long Beach, California, US, 1997, Rios Associates with WWCOT

Rather than hide an ungainly collection of upturned satellite dishes, the icons of global communication became the focus of the arrival area. The initial impetus for the scheme, designed in collaboration with architects WWCOT, came from several sources. First, the practical: the company's sizeable satellite dishes had to be accommodated near the headquarters. Second, management wanted to herald the company's success in the field of satellite communications. Add to that the emotional and the playful: an urge to shut out the overbearing and overdeveloped character of the surrounding fringe-city. And, why not have fun doing so?

Andrea Gehring of WWCOT recalls that she really had to sell the idea of the dishes as industrial sculpture that, when placed in an attractive environment, would be considered beautiful, and when given a functional identity, such as an entry courtyard, would be seen as inviting. To give the proposal a conceptual framework, Mark Rios researched imagery from ancient civilizations' communications with the heavens, for example, the prehistoric ruin of Stonehenge in Wiltshire, UK.

Set between the parking lots and the building's main entry, the arrival court is a simple rectangle within a circle. Within this configuration, functional items, such as security fencing, are perceived as integral elements of the site geometry. Much of the ancillary equipment that frequently surrounds high-tech installations was eliminated to maximize the dishes' sculptural qualities. There is a sense, notes Rios, that it is OK for people to coexist with technology.

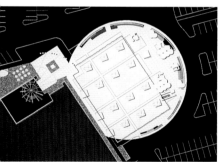

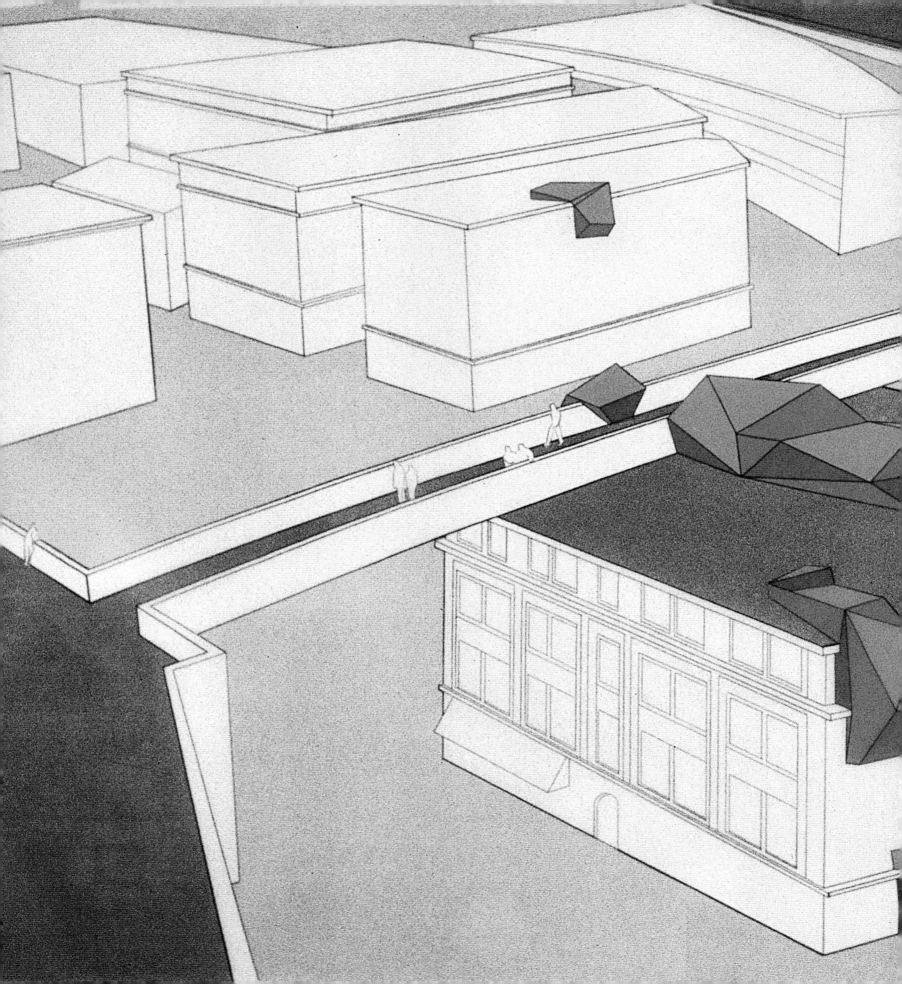

WHEN ECOLOGY PREYS ON THE CITY
Les Jardins Mutants
Switzerland, 1999, Ken Smith Landscape Architect

Material specifications for this proposal include: galvanized-steel-pipe armatures, chain-link fencing, lightweight soil, grow lights and 'aggressive fast-growing pernicious vines'. Landscape architect Ken Smith challenges the established norm of the 'jardin urbain', by proposing that nature has been supplanted by infrastructure as the shaping force in urban landscapes. Smith's 'fresh design strategies' incorporate the idea that 'infrastructure in and of itself operates as a determinant (of new urban gardens) in a kind of transgressive ecological process of growth, decline, renewal, and replication'.

Mutant gardens are hermaphroditic landscapes, a guerrilla typology that is neither wholly cultivated nature nor built structure. The hybrid entities are opportunistic, adapting the (perhaps unwilling) host's form and growth patterns, exploiting weaknesses in the infrastructural ecology. In Platform du Flon (shown here), the mutant garden organism colonizes an abandoned industrial warehouse. The parasitic growth is composed of low-tech standard construction materials and of weed-species vines.

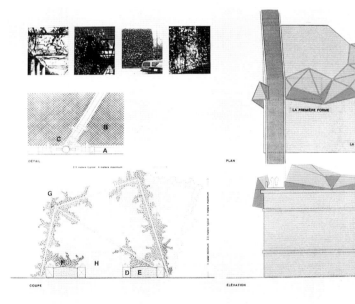

EQUILIBRIUM AT THE SEAM OF EARTH AND WATER
Jellyfish I, II and III
Various locations, 1990–, Makoto Sei Watanabe

A hybrid of a different sort, architect and visionary Makoto Sei Watanabe's Jellyfish project explores the balance of opposites. The series is a prototype for experimenting with the fundamental properties of light and water. Equilibrium versus instability, transparency versus opacity, contraction versus expansion – the juxtaposition of these complementary forces gives form, motion and meaning to Jellyfish. Each version of the project is perched on an edge where land meets water; the first is a seaside holiday home, the second a waterfront museum, the third (pictured here) a guest pavilion on a tiny island in a vast lake.

Watanabe is fascinated by water. 'It gives things wings,' he says, pointing out that on land we can only move backward and forward and side to side, but in water, we are buoyant and move in whichever direction we choose. Watanabe is charmed by light in water: water serves as a filter that alters the wavelength, reflectivity and transmissivity of light. Furthermore, he points out that it is in water that true three-dimensionality is apparent. The ultimate goal of Jellyfish is to 'exchange substance for space and space for substance', to question the notion that space is empty and substance is dense.

Jellyfish is a mechanism of measurement. The dwelling's primary living space is located in the foundation, which is also the base for the giant scales. At one end is a volume of fluid, appearing to be cut out of the sea, at the other end sits 'a hardened piece of atmosphere'. As the day heats up and cools off, the two bodies change consistency and weight. Equilibrium occurs only momentarily.

A NEW KIND OF FOREST
Kuala Lumpur International Airport + Eco-Media City
Malaysia, 1998, Kisho Kurokawa

The phrase, 'an airport in the forest, a forest in
the airport' won architect and thinker Kisho
Kurokawa the 1992 competition for Kuala Lumpur's
international airport. The site is cut out of a
24,710-acre (10,000 hectares) tree plantation
adjacent to an urban area, and there really is a forest
in the airport: at the centre of the Satellite Building
is a circular void, a well that will one day be brimming
with foliage that will be seen from all concourses.
The architect hopes to establish links with the
primeval forest body by cloaking façades, filling
courtyards and surrounding infrastructure with dense
native plantings. Mimicking the biodiversity of the
rainforest, eighty-six species of trees, thirteen
varieties of palm, forty kinds of shrubs, three types
of bamboo and a variety of rock formations are
featured. A detailed landscape succession plan is in
place to guide the neo-forest's evolution, ensuring
that it matures to integrate into and extend out of the
airport's architectural form. Twelve acres (5 hectares)
of cleared plantation have been set aside as an
experimental forest nursery. →

→ Kurokawa sees the airport complex as a manifestation of the potential for synthesis. He envisions an 'eco-media city', a place where nature, technology and humankind are in harmony. The design of the airport illustrates the idea of technology as architecture as nature, because its structural system evokes a forest with sky above. The role of the technological metaphor and the substitution of artificial for biological forest was described in <u>Domus</u> (no. 808): 'In the departure lounge the roof is formed by grandiose parabolic pyramids .... Zig-zag paths wind through the truncated cone pillars as far as the eye can see, and their depth is deceptive .... We [think of] an architectural forest, where young shoots poke their noses out of the floor, and others grow tall enough to hold up the starry sky above (the ceiling lamps are arranged in a random pattern) .... This landscape dynamically exploits the metamorphosis of architectural figures, yet leans on the precision of technology and drawing.'

RAISING THE PEOPLE, CHANGING PERCEPTION
Treetop Walk
Walpole-Nornalup National Park, Australia, 1996, Donaldson + Warn (architects), David Jones (environmental artist)

On the extreme southwest edge of Australia lies an 'ancient empire' – the world's last surviving forest of giant red tingle trees (Eucalyptus jacksonii), red-flowering gums (Eucalyptus ficifolia) and the majestic white-trunked karri (Eucalyptus diversicolor). Suffering from insufficient facilities to accommodate heavy and increasing tourist traffic, the forest was in danger of being over-loved. In response to a request from the Department of Conservation and Land Management (CALM), collaborators Donaldson + Warn and David Jones devised the Treetop Walk to keep visitors off the forest floor and to improve handicap accessibility.

A delicate overhead structure, according to the designers, was inspired by 'the form of understory species of sword grass and tassel flower' and is lightly poised within the dense forest. Six sections, each 197 feet (60 metres) long, interlock at a series of widened nodes that provide perches for visitors to pause and observe the tree canopy. The walkway threads through the towering tingle-tree and karri canopy – up to 131 feet (40 metres) high – delivering an eco-adrenaline experience not soon forgotten, while simultaneously allowing the forest floor to regenerate. Over 20,000 visitors experience the unique view each year, indicating that nature-based tourism continues to gain popularity.

FASHION VICTIM OR VISIONARY?
Hair Gardens
Photomontage series, 1998, Ken Smith
Landscape Architect

So, what <u>do</u> hair care and garden design have in common? Ken Smith answers, 'They are both organic, grow and are willfully manipulated. They have to do with social display, fashion, and pretence, and share many related artistic concerns and cultural attitudes.' Always exploring the symbolic content and expressive power of the landscape, Smith responded to an invitation to participate in 'The Very Hairy Show' at the Max Fish gallery. He executed a series of photomontages with such names as 'Ear Hair Rockery', 'Eyebrow Perennial Border', 'Underarm Herb Garden', 'Pubic Shade Garden' and, pictured below, 'Bouffant Topiary' and 'Chest Hair Maze'.

The artist claims that he borrows coiffure techniques – and the related fashion imagery – as a means to envision new garden typologies. However, as Smith is aware, it is about more than just spending hard-earned money and valuable time on the cultivation of lawn-, garden- and hair-styling. It is also about the intense emotional investment that they represent. A richly blossoming shrub in the front garden is a source of pride for the whole family. A bad-hair day reflects the depths of our inner soul.

LIVING MEMORY
Vivaio Per La Pace (Nursery for Peace)
Pistoia, Italy, 1999, Dani Karavan

Dani Karavan has been described as a constructor between memory and continuity. He is also a sculptor of space and a director of images. Karavan's work is simultaneously site-specific and temporally equivocal. Living in Tel Aviv and Paris (where he has a studio), Karavan creates installations that speak of the earth's metaphysical qualities, our histories and our cultural stories. His work resonates in cities around the world, including Beer Sheba, Cologne, Duisburg, Florence, Port Bou, Sapporo, Seoul, Venice and Zurich. Italo Moscati of the Centro per l'Arte Contemporanea Luigi Pecci in Italy describes Karavan's work as events that go beyond common experience, spectacular confrontations between environment and creativity. →

→ In the small city of Pistoia's Piazza del Duomo, the core of the urban construct, Karavan plants fragments of childhood memories and weaves together threads of the local culture in a call for world peace. Having a landscape designer as a father who once installed an arbour in the family atrium, Karavan developed a symbolic tree palette, collected and presented on a wood-plank platform, as a means to reference the nursery traditions of the region. Perhaps the idea of a nursery for peace is whimsical, but philosophically it has deep roots and robust associations. Notions of the value of shared resources, variety within unity, the miracle and fragility of life and the shrinking nature of our global ecology are all present.

Karavan's scheme is a personal story, a celebration of the city's nursery tradition and an international call for peace.

Aerial view of the Schiphol Airport Garden

STRATEGIC INFILL FOR THE FUTURE
Schiphol Airport Garden
The Netherlands, 1998, West 8 Landscape Architects

Charged with relandscaping the rapidly expanding Schiphol airport, West 8 decided upon a simple strategy: the systematic planting of birches in all empty and unused spaces. Pre-existing ornamental shrubs were excavated and replaced with pure groves of birch rising off an uncluttered ground plane of clover. The bright-green clover fixes the nutrient nitrogen and is resown continually by bees whose hives are watched over by the airport beekeeper.

Each season, 25,000 trees are planted and the designers envision a future where the hulking airport mass 'is put into perspective by the green haze' of foliage. On a macro-scale, it is anticipated that the monocultural installation will bind the sprawling airport into a coherent enclave at the south axis of Amsterdam. Regionally, the green element becomes a node within a string of 'green cores' along the Schiphol ring road.

West 8 designed several specific sites within the airport complex, including monolithic stone arrangements that enliven the space between parking and circulation decks; a location for plane spotters; and the Jan Dellaert Square at the entrance to the arrival and departure hall. A concern with linking the site to others on a national level and the degree of elegance in planting and construction detailing, perhaps sets a precedent for places of public transportation. The use of landscaping to engage the visitor beyond the notion of a surface on which to stub out a cigarette or a curb from which to hail a taxi, signals a remarkably positive step toward asserting regional aesthetics in the face of global standardization of our built environment. (See pp. 106–107.)

GARDENS FOR EXPLORATION
Festival International des Jardins,
Chaumont-sur-Loire, France, 1996–99,
various designers

[this page] **Sillon Romand** Designed in 1996
by Daniel Ortli of Lausanne, Switzerland.
Vertical mirrors reflect contrasting garden
types as each furrow is planted with an urban
palette on one side and a rural mix on the
other. The vegetal selection represents Ortli's
take on 'the strictly policed urban environment'
and the 'explosive generosity of the country'.

[opposite top] **Potager Dansant** Designed
by festival students and trainees in 1999, this
is 'a dancing vegetable garden', with allusions
to the floating gardens of Mexico. A system
of pipes is used to direct water currents so
that reed rafts with their growing cargo swirl
across the pool.

[opposite bottom] **From Sky to Earth**
Designed in 1999 by Takano Landscape
Planning, Japan, three spirals collect
water that comes up from the ground
or falls from the sky. Run-off eventually
gathers at the centre of the plot, alluding
to the cycle of water.

No longer is the idea of context an implication of local proximity. Materials, arrangements and forms that constitute a space may refer to and be taken from geographically, ecologically and culturally far-flung sources.

Urban

ngredients

There is a significant body of contemporary urban landscape design that strives to promote a progressive dialogue with the city on behalf of man and nature.

The making of a human environment ... now goes beyond the idea of something finite or established. Experience is leading us towards another dimension. **Paulo Mendes da Rocha**[1]

Green infrastructure has long played a vital role in the urban environment. When linked together in a coherent pattern, such individual landscape elements as the allée or promenade, the plaza or town green, the parkway or boulevard compose a living network that offers social, ecological and functional resources. As our cities change we sometimes see a corresponding shift in landscape prototypes. But, often not – traditional forms and symbolic content are remarkably persistent in the face of evolving urbanism, resulting in a disjunction between new and old that renders landscape as background, as infill, as mute in the face of emerging trends.

In the urban realm, the term 'garden' is becoming more and more flexible. Within a regional framework, a city becomes a garden: urban blocks are beds, cycles and patterns of growth are evident in the tended versus untended precincts. In short, it is an organic entity encompassing many divergent but interactive parts within the whole, distinct from the surrounding environment, integrated by a shared exchange of energy and resources. On a more localized level, outdoor spaces of an intimate scale – paved or planted, private or public – are an inherent, critical punctuation in the city's rhythm of space.

Radical place-makers of today operate on all these levels, providing essential city ingredients. In the condensed Netherlands, some planning firms focus on 'corridor formation', particularly in the sectors becoming rapidly urbanized between Rotterdam's World Port, Schiphol Airport, and the Ring Cities. Issues of home and work, recreation, energy production and water management dominate, as new process-based models of synthesized urban/rural landscapes emerge. A 'nationwide ecological structure ... adapted to the needs of modern land use yet in harmony with natural processes' is proposed in an 'era of decadence, virtuosity, alienation, and estrangement' in which 'discoveries' are manifest side-by-side with a 'return to the source, the womb of Mother Nature, in the age of the search for meaning'.[2]

In Barcelona, landscape architects, garden designers, architects, engineers and urban planners are reworking the historic city fabric in raiments of woven urban ecologies. According to the journalist Hanno Rauterberg, 'new elements are to be found all over the place,' the city is no longer regarded as 'an integral, controllable entity, but rather as a system made up of other systems, many of them overlapping, subject to constant change, even contradictory in nature, and thus requiring customized

solutions as a way of introducing the new.'[3] The design of open space/ green infrastructure as the underpinning of urban revitalization is an important notion in today's built landscapes. Geographer Jordi Borja describes Barcelona's focus on neighbourhood-oriented improvements as acupunctural in character.

Under very different circumstances, the same notion was explored by a loose coalition of architects and artists at Bloemenhof Park in Johannesburg (p. 136). The group viewed the site as a potentially positive urban node within a fragile part of town. It was, possibly, an opportunity to turn the threat of loss into the promise of play. After observing conditions surrounding the square, a set of features was identified that would be recreationally useful to the local underprivileged population. The park scheme focuses upon a skating structure – an open-form concrete bowl that welcomes graffiti and other forms of public interaction. Imagery from the city backdrop was transposed directly onto the bowl by painting a fragment of a distant Coca-Cola billboard onto the raised lip. Urban grit – both in image and in material – personify the park. The place is threatened, endangered by political forces much stronger than the community of users who value its presence, even given the bare minimum of amenities. The project raises an interesting ambiguity that haunts our public spaces: at what point does a much-used, much-needed patch of ground in a neighbourhood gain support, and then funding, as a legitimate expression of civic values? How many others languish and decay for lack of influential constituents?

At the Macon Yards project in Georgia (p. 146), Hood Design attempts to simultaneously address the encompassing city structure and the very localized neighbourhood interaction. By accepting the block divisions of the site, allowing each to express its own use and character (the programme includes a civic yard, a market yard, a music yard, a children's yard, among others), and by linking the parts into a cohesive whole, Walter Hood plays out urban ideals that are often forgotten on developers' drawing boards. He faces the challenge of defining levels of public access, from open space to semi-private spaces, without isolating any of the areas. The scheme started with the thought that the back yard is where 'all the bad stuff' is hidden, and set out to exploit and reverse this idea. Parking, an urban necessity that we would like to sweep under the rug with the rusting stuff in our back yards, is integrated into the design and acknowledged as an integrative action in the urban system.

Green infrastructure is a social tool, perhaps most vehemently within the urban setting, where it takes on invisible implications of cultural symbolism in addition to its physical manifestation. In the past decade, 'a shift away from spatial and aesthetic categories, away from terms which were supposed to describe shapes and feelings towards them' has been noted. And, similarly to buildings of the 1980s and 1990s, landscapes that read as signs carrying ideological messages have lost ground to place-making 'as networks where people move and interact, as platforms' where aspirations are acted out.[4]

1 Mendes da Rocha, Paulo. 'Consolidating a Site'. Pages Paysages (no. 8, 00/01): 91.
2 9+1: 10 Young Dutch Landscape Architecture Firms (Rotterdam: NAi Publishers, 1999).
3 Rauterberg, Hanno. 'Reconquering Barcelona'. Topos (Munich: Callwey München, vol. 29, 12/99).
4 Lefaivre, Liane and Alexander Tzonis. Architecture in Europe Since 1968: Memory and Invention (London: Thames & Hudson and New York: Rizzoli, 1992).

SURVIVAL OF THE FITTEST
Bloemenhof Park
Johannesburg, South Africa, 1998, Fiona Garson, Jan Hofmeyr,
Hannah le Roux (park concept). Sarah Calburn and
Rodney Place (rink design)

In a series of community workshops, architects Fiona Garson,
Jan Hofmeyr and Hannah le Roux developed a plan for the
renovation of a neighbourhood park in Troyeville, a mixed-race
inner-city residential suburb of Johannesburg. Local architect
Sarah Calburn and artist Rodney Place of z.a.r. works were
brought in to design the largest component of the park, a
skateboard rink. While a limited budget and political difficulties
hindered full realization of the project, the rink and other
eccentric touches rarely found in an urban park were completed.
For example, Filipe Fernandes's humanoid benches, Larry le
Roux's welded wart-hog barbecues and Andrew Lindsay's vivid
mosaic inhabit sloped stretches of the dry ground.

Calburn describes the park as a rough environment in
which 'down and outers get displaced by the tough kids, who
get displaced by the homeless'. Entitled 'City Bowl', the rink is
the only one of its kind in the area. Calburn and Place, fearing
that the park was a receding layer of the city in danger of
peeling off, forged a visual connection between the rink and
the business core of Johannesburg by appropriating 'a certain
iconic view' glimpsed from the park. 'As an instantly relatable
and humourous landscape piece', the team applied a →

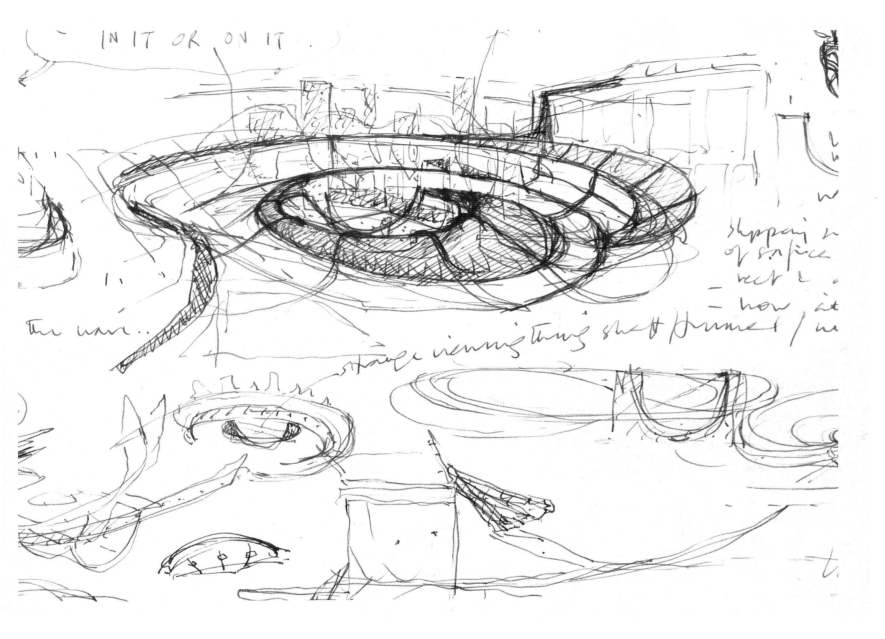

IN IT OR ON IT

At what point does a much-used, much-needed patch of ground in a neighbourhood become a legitimate expression of civic values?

→ slice of a Coca-Cola logo to the inside of the bowl, echoing the bold red-and-white advertisement seen in the distance atop an office tower.

Bald patches exist in the centre of the concrete bowl, where the lack of funding prevented the installation of grass, but the barbecue in the guise of a grazing wart-hog waits there all the same. Promises of trees and other plantings have not materialized, but skateboarders gather there every day. Calburn says that in Johannesburg, 'gardens are things behind walls in the suburbs, and public gardens from the old days are contested', which makes one wonder whether, in her mind, true 'public space' can be realized in this city, in these times. She sees the spectres of fear and exclusion as dominant spatial informers on today's streets. The City Bowl, therefore, is a work of urban discourse, not just in its functional concave form, but in the inherent symbolism of its shared terrain and open stature.

Intended as an amenity for residents who wanted play space for their children, the upgrade of Bloemenhof Park is now referred to as 'a social sink' of decay and low civic morale. The earnest creativity of the architects and artists, who, for a time, planted this place with art, recreation and humour, is in grave jeopardy. (See pp. 132–33.)

[left] ANIMATING THE URBAN FABRIC
HAT Kobe Wakinohama
Kobe, Japan, 1997, Yoji Sasaki

The walkway within a new housing complex is a small part of a project envisioned as 'an arrangement of spaces somehow indicative of community life, achieved through a combination of court-type open spaces and street-like open spaces'. The construction celebrates the rebirth of Kobe after the 1995 earthquake. Housing blocks are linked by a system of alleys and wide pedestrian streets. These elements, or connective tissues, are tempered with paving, planting and lighting that provide the 'animation of urban housing' and 'a sense of psychological security'. Seen here, 'fire-fly' lights on decking at night.

KNITTING THE PAST INTO THE FUTURE
Yokohama Portside Park
Japan, 1999, Hiroki Hasegawa/Studio on Site

Along Yokohama's waterfront a new city of mixed-use development is rising up to replace outmoded industrial infrastructure. Imagery and materials from the site's past and from neighbouring areas are incorporated into the park, and although in new form or put to novel use, Hasegawa hopes that each piece expresses its own distinctive character that relates the item to its source.

Lawn mounds, cobblestone paving, steel members, wild vegetation, wood decks and brick plazas together have contemporary purpose, but on an individual basis retain reference to earlier manifestations. The design statement reads 'Components are without exception significant keys to any landscape, but the most important thing is that each one is full of meaning, like a symbolic word .... The difference between the things that are inserted into the landscape is only slight, but each one acts as a catalyst.'

The park is composed of successive layers [right]: earthwork (linear berms that run the length of the site and parallel to the waterfront), trees (strategically placed rows call out circulation routes), paving (paths link urban fabric to pedestrian streets within the park) and site objects (benches, lighting, etc.). →

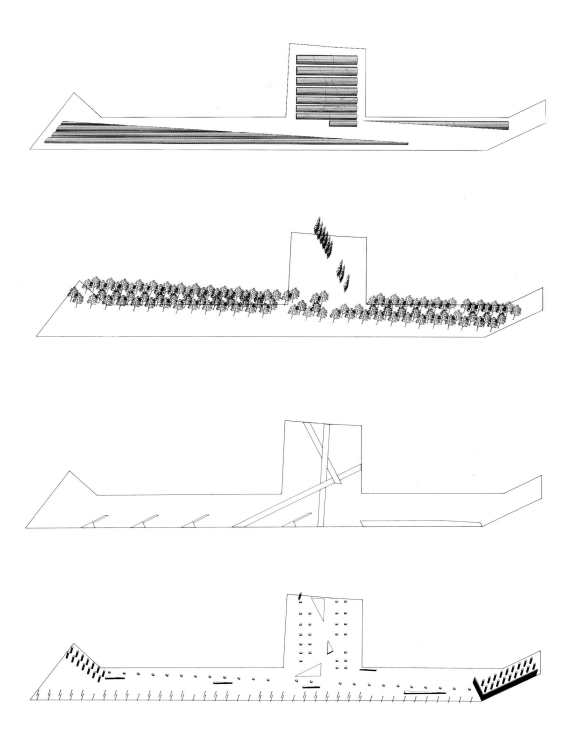

→ The park has a concise language that lets both urban and ocean currents be heard. There is no overt boundary to the site, nor, according to the project statement, a 'firm image'. Visitors are expected to relate to different aspects of the place, depending on time of day and other variables. The park's entrance is flanked by the moulded, sliced grass mounds that grow smaller as they undulate toward the waterline. A 1312-foot (400 metres) double row of elm trees runs the length of the shoreline promenade; wood decks extrude out over the water at regular intervals. Along the shoreline, native reeds and grasses have been restored and are protected by a system of pre-cast concrete blocks that hold soil and break wave energy.

COMMUNITY EXPRESSION
Edward Square
Islington, London, UK, 2000, J+L Gibbons Landscape

Layers of site history and an awareness of diverse community needs are revealed in the scheme for Edward Square. The project statement outlines an unusually in-depth collaborative effort between the design team, the community and the Local Authority. For example, various types of seating are specifically designed to serve different user groups, and a grouping of ornamental crab trees complement a pre-existing, well-loved apple tree. Brick paths are made from original nineteenth-century materials unearthed on site, and the cobbled walkways are the original roads into the square. Boulders from Inverness-shire display aspects of geological metamorphosis and are arranged in a radiating pattern around an oak tree to create an informal outdoor classroom.

MARKING THE CAMPUS
Deusto University Courtyard
Bilbao, Spain, 1990, Fernando Caruncho
A labyrinth of basalt stone occupies one side of
the campus courtyard. Both a sculptural object
and a spatial organizer, the stonework is striking
in the urban context for its powerful symbolism
that is open to many interpretations. Boxwood
(Buxus sempervirens) provides a green edge
to the courtyard without softening the chiselled
bas-relief of the architectural space.

Outdoor spaces – paved
or planted, private or
public – provide essential
city ingredients.

TRACING URBAN CHANGE
Courtland Creek
Oakland, California, US, 1997, Hood Design

In the amalgamation of park, street, urban infrastructure and wilderness, a multilayered framework draws attention to the quirks and history of the host neighbourhood. A double row of 150 trees parades over five blocks, marking the bed of a defunct train corridor. In Hood's estimation, the formal allée stands out because it is a construct rarely seen in low-income neighbourhoods such as this. The atypical character of the allée also stems from the choice of tree species – the purple-leaf plum is very unlike the trees that normally line streets and was selected for its intimate scale, instant impact after installation and distinct seasonal changes. Sporadic placements of public art mark pre-existing features – community gardens, basketball courts, creekside picnic areas – that occur at certain nodes along the pedestrian way. The overlapping configuration of repeating linear typologies – street, railroad, riparian corridor and allée – establishes an uncommonly strong, unifying gesture across the multivalent cityscape.

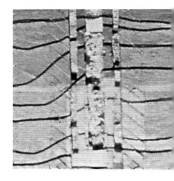

[right, opposite top right and bottom] **PSYCHOLOGICAL ARCHAEOLOGY IN THE PUBLIC REALM**
Macon Yards
Macon, Georgia, US, 2000, Hood Design

Urban landscape architect Walter Hood won a competition to improve a 180-foot-wide (54.9 metres) boulevard in the heart of downtown Macon. His entry was based on two fundamental ideas: first, the observation that the backyard is where people 'hide the bad stuff'; second, the notion that this paradigm would be interesting to reverse. He began a process of psychological archaeology, of uncovering aspects of local urban history through research and community focus groups. Issues of gentrification and conflicting use were examined, with a vision of the yards – although acknowledged to be both common and contested ground – as an ultimately public realm.

In Hood's scheme, the Poplar Street right-of-way is divided into six yards, each with its own character, ranging from archetypal typologies (civic and market yards that relate to adjacent historic buildings), to site-specific themes (the creek and geology), to the more highly programmed spaces (children and music). By retaining the layout of city blocks, the linear site becomes an intrinsic part of the city fabric. Hood created a series of cross-sectional studies and a segmented site model [right].

Implemented in a less-than-thriving part of Macon, the project is expected to revive the area by attracting mixed-use redevelopment. Pedestrian and car circulation are major priorities: parking occurs in the yards, mixing street life with automobile circulation as two sides of the same coin. Public transit runs between the yards. This is a key point of Hood's design; it is a fresh solution to the foot traffic versus vehicle access conflict that plagues many urban districts today. Macon Yards is a contemporary take on the pedestrian-mall model that has been so popular in recent decades. It is 'a hybrid of street/yard/urban infrastructure … a series of outdoor yards that house new street amenities and means of social interaction.'

Walter Hood meets the challenge of defining levels of public access, from open space to semi-private space, without isolating any of the areas.

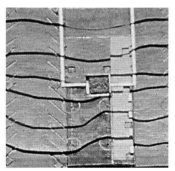

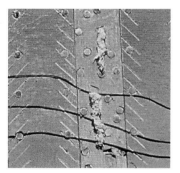
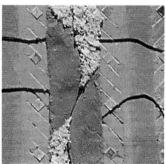

PERPETUAL EVOLUTION
Eerste Marnixplantsoen
Amsterdam, The Netherlands, 1997, Eker en Schaap
Partners Mark Eker and Joram Schaap begin with the
simple fact that the landscape constantly changes.
By definition, a landscape design can propose only
a temporary condition. The renovation of the small
Marnixplantsoen urban park in Amsterdam's city centre
offers multiple layers upon which different activities
are combined. The flexible approach includes an
underground café that at night illuminates the playing
fields above and a sculptural bridge.

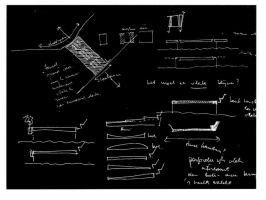

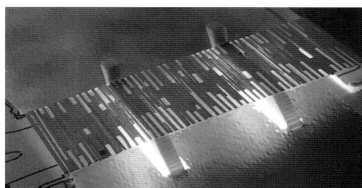

The design of open space/green infrastructure
is the underpinning of urban revitalization

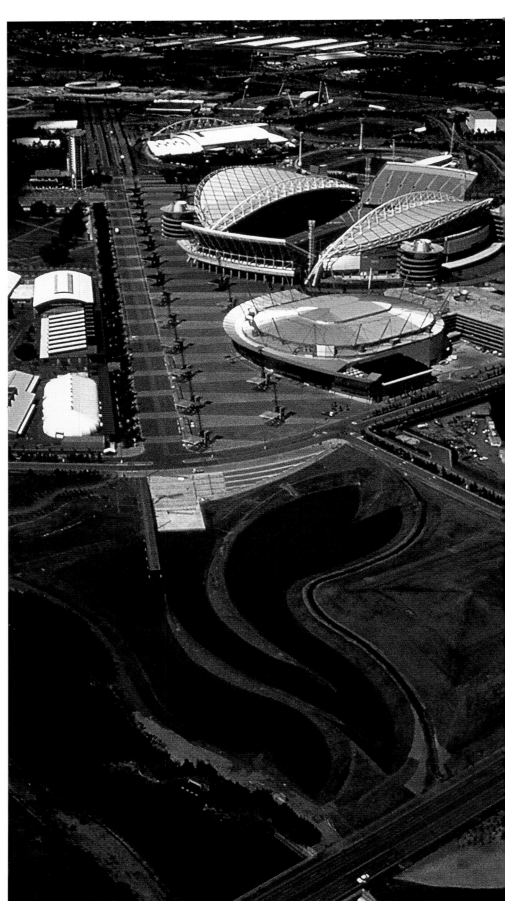

ECOLOGY AS SPECTACLE AND CONTENT
Northern Water Feature 2000
Sydney Olympics Campus, Homebush Bay,
Australia, 2000, Hargreaves Associates

A signature landscape and high-profile environmental rescue, Hargreaves Associates' masterplan for the redevelopment of Homebush Bay for the 2000 Olympics eloquently links storm-water management and urban design within a landscape that celebrates ecology, recreation and commerce. The commission adds to the firm's growing list of eco-civic projects and explores the potential of design as a dynamic manipulation of natural systems. Three design gestures bring organizational clarity to the 741-acre (300 hectares) Urban Core: the Red Move, a central, paved, open space known as the Olympic Plaza; the Green Move, a landscape framework of 'fingers' that thread through the site; and the Blue Move, a visible infrastructure that uses the process of

storm-water collection, cleansing and re-use to instil order and narrative, and to symbolically connect neighbouring river systems and Homebush Bay. A major element of the Blue Move, the curvilinear bays of the Northern Water Feature terminate one end of the Olympic Plaza. Radiating granite terraces, doubling as observation decks, step down to meet a constructed wetland. Thirty-three-foot-high (10 metres) arcs of water soar from three angled banks of attenuated cones, aerating and showcasing at the same time. Varying moisture gradients at the water's edge display working patterns of plant life. The project transforms typically invisible systems of storm-water management into an emblematic landscape, one in which ecology becomes a spectator sport.

STAGING URBAN INTERACTION
Motomachi CRED Fureai Plaza and Sky Patio
Hiroshima City, Japan, 1994, Yoji Sasaki

Hotel and commercial areas in the centre of Hiroshima City form a three-dimensional corridor or 'promenade in the sky'. Visitors move between the Sky Patio, a broad roof terrace on the sixth level, and the street-level Fureai Plaza. The lower level is paved in a pattern of varying textures to represent the nearby Inland Sea, and, at the same time, Sasaki hopes that the objectified, activated ground plane will create a dynamic atmosphere to attract shoppers. The Sky Patio holds a circular, striped Mist Stage set against the backdrop of the city and the distant mountains. A monumental staircase gives the impression of exposed architecture, as if this were once a grand interior suddenly revealed by the removal of exterior walls.

Sites
Tell
Stories

All landscapes are underpinned by a personal history. Some are designed to relay specific messages about culture, ecology, people and place.

> Designing gardens means experiencing stories. Stories may have an end, while gardens are never completed. In this sense, our garden stories - at least the good ones - don't have an end but new chapters are always being added to them.
>
> **Dieter Kienast**[1]

Gardens and landscapes are fingerprints of our cultural experience. Layer upon layer of clues to our most basic and our loftiest pursuits exist in all settings, from rural agricultural lands to wilderness reaches to urban shores. As economies shift, policies are inaugurated and technologies developed that deeply affect our built environment. Pragmatism and aesthetics work in tandem at times and are coldly divorced at others. As a society we are constantly reshaping terrain, delving into or attempting to replenish our biological resources and reinventing our environment in our own image. Place-making, or manipulation of place, is a game humankind plays out within the dynamic confines of ecosystems and urban networks.

The site is a key to its own history, which in itself is a product of the interworkings and mechanics of nested mega-myths. The site also tells legends and perpetrates communal myths that tend to bind a population with shared beliefs and expectations. Because of these phenomena, when man intercedes in the landscape there is an ever-present choice: to eradicate or to augment the existing. Both are acts of interpretation, invention and modification that require comprehension of the past and vision for the future.

For many forward-looking place-makers of today, the value of a site's story is more important than formal and compositional concerns. Site order is an internal force, not always readily visible. One must learn about the project and its story before understanding how and why the pieces fit together. Although they share a consciously didactic bent, the gardens shown in this chapter are not one-liners that present a narrative of imposed signs, symbols and tools of information. The designers have based initial concepts, programmatic choices and site structure on the revelation of specific ideas, but do not rely on conventional modes of communication to convey this message. Often, the message is about a long-term process, such as water circulation as a cleansing mechanism; or an unpredictable condition, such as watershed fluctuations; or an invisible or intangible agent, such as peace. To relay information, the designers incorporate natural elements of the site context – either human behavioural or ecological/meteorological – into their built landscapes that resonate with visitors on multiple levels.

The Office of Cheryl Barton sifted through remnants of past site activities and incorporated particularly evocative elements for a new campus masterplan at the obsolete Presidio Military Base in San Francisco. From a crumbling red concrete curb segment to the footprints of razed buildings, the Thoreau Center for Sustainability (p. 170) stitches old and new together into a legible site plan that can be experienced and used viscerally, or studied and understood as a cultural tale. But the centre not only brings added meaning to historical circumstances with its new water-harvesting infrastructure, it also showcases opportunities for the integration of sustainable site design within urban and post-industrial areas. According to the designer's statement, the scheme has a tripartite ambition 'to mediate between the competing philosophies of sustainable site/building design and cultural landscape preservation and interpretation; to demonstrate that a sustainable landscape does not have to be an invisible landscape; to celebrate the power and significance of water'.

In 'Mimmamakin' (From the Depth) at a defunct coal plant in Germany's Ruhr Valley (p. 176), Dani Karavan chose to create a sculptural statement from abandoned equipment and evidence of a ravaged landscape. Bruno Cora, artistic director at the Centro per l'Arte Contemporanea Luigi Pecci in Prato (Italy), describes Karavan's intense gardens of dust, earth, concrete, water, light and memory as 'an eloquent synthesis [that] becomes the vehicle to communicate that which is mute but that impresses itself strongly in the individual conscience'. There is 'an explicit meditative quality, inducing the observer into a complex experience,'[2] going beyond the parameters of site and time.

While meditative qualities and the persistence of place-based memory are certainly accounted for in PLANT's Sweet Farm project (p. 164), they are achieved by quite different means. At a remote estate in Quebec, the design team invested significant time and study into a survey of existing factors, quirks and conditions in the landscape. A 'forest garden', brought about by 'a different kind of gardening', was conceived to emphasize happenstance encounters within the 85-acre (34 hectares) sylvan site. Gems and germs of past lives, found lodged within the overgrowth, are left as icons of waning productivity, changing times, humankind's acceptance of nature as a partner and our disregard of no longer useful items. An abandoned car, a tangle of rusting barbed wire, a stack of foreboding mink traps, deteriorating parts of a hundred-year-old logging operation are woven tenuously into, or alongside, a series of pathways that slice through typical sectors of the terrain. Writer Tony Hiss states that 'the sweetness of Sweet Farm is that it fully displays the astounding beauty of the landscape. The discreteness of Sweet Farm is the subtle way it blends reverence and ruthlessness, to make us aware of our kinship with a forest that is busy healing itself, and with the generations of people who passed through the woods, using it, abusing it, and then vanishing, leaving it to its own devices.'[3]

Sites tell stories as a result of accretion. Shapers of the landscape peel back onionlike layers of a site's history, seemingly opaque but translucent once freed from the growing body. What seed was planted to bring these landscapes to life, and how will they be tended?

1 Kienast, Dieter. Kienast-Gardens (Berlin: Birkhäuser, 1998).
2 Cora, Bruno. 'Dani Karavan: Construction Between Memory and Continuity'. Dani Karavan (catalogue for exhibition at Fort Belvedere in Florence, 1999): 33–38.
3 Hiss, Tony. 'Increasing the Volume'. Gardens Illustrated (February 1999).

Sites Tell Stories

ACTING OUT PURIFICATION
Living Water Park
Chengdu, China, 1999, Betsy Damon, Margie Ruddick and the
FuNan Rivers Renovation Bureau

Charged with creating a park alongside a polluted river that brings issues of water quality and cleansing methods to the forefront of urban experience, artist Betsy Damon and landscape architect Margie Ruddick, who prepared the design in collaboration with the project team, saw their roles as organizers of a discovery process. Rather than imposing a formal solution from the outset, the two met with representatives from numerous city agencies and allowed parts of the puzzle to evolve in a compositionally independent manner. Working closely with aquatic engineers and microbiologists, the designers developed a chain of biological filtering devices. As the living medium of water passes through flow forms, aeration surfaces and constructed wetlands, its various treatments become a structuring device for the park.

The park is both an ecological mechanism and a public amenity. Interaction with the filter zones is encouraged through various types of circulation: a boardwalk alongside the wetlands brings visitors and native vegetation face to face; stepping stones lead the curious across a settling pool; a plaza frames the symbolic fountainhead. The park serves as a model that will educate and perhaps inspire similar projects. Ruddick sees the work, which was a collaboration between many designers and scientists, as being more about living systems than about creating a single, visible order on the land.

CULTURAL MEMORY IN CIVIC SPACE
The Page, Lindenstrasse Memorial
Berlin, Germany, 1996, Zvi Hecker

Notions and notations of memory and cultural history are
embedded in Zvi Hecker's site designs. In Berlin, The Page
memorializes a synagogue destroyed during Kristallnacht on the
night of 10 November 1938. As visitors take respite in the grass
courtyard, they are reminded of events beyond their sphere of
experience: rows of concrete benches are built in the precise
location of the original wood prayer benches, testifying to the
loss of the building and a community. The lines are broken to
resemble Talmudic text, and trees and bushes that grew over
the ruins have been left to punctuate the script (see pp. 154–55).

Created in collaboration with Micha Ullman and Eyal Weizman,
The Page is a three-layered composite of time and metaphor: the
benches, spectres of incinerated pews and a defunct congregation;
the 'volunteer' vegetation, nature's response to the act of
destruction; and the emergency vehicle access road that crosses
the site, a mark of contemporary building requirements. Together,
says Hecker, these elements form a holy script, 'Walking the
narrow passages between the lines becomes an act of reading.
This is a story of loss.'

Our work is a page of a book
telling a 100-year history of
a piece of land .... We have
added nothing to the site that
had not been there before.'

SITE, EVENT, MEMORY, REBIRTH
Fire Garden
Malibu, California, US, 1994, Pamela Burton

A landscape architect concerned with the history of
landscape and the creation of architectural spaces
that have symbolic resonance, Pamela Burton was
put in the unusual position of applying professional
philosophy to a very personal event. Burton watched
her house and 130 acres (52 hectares) of land burn in
the Malibu fires, and was nearly caught by a 200-foot
(61 metres) tongue of fire. In the aftermath, she
envisioned a garden about ashes and rejuvenation.
It is set in a rectangular earthen room, with a floor
of hard-packed, blackened, decomposed granite.
The entry path is aligned with the sunrise on the
vernal equinox, a literal connection to the mythic
power of spring as a time of new beginnings. A tight
grid of singed yucca pineapples covers the space,
interspersed with scorched sumac root crowns.
A pair of Phoenix palms, trunks charred, marks
one end of the room and frames the rising equinox
sun. Brilliantly coloured new growth on the plants
becomes the focal point of the garden, representing
the return of life after cataclysm and acknowledging
the transformational power of fire.

INTO THE FOLD
L'Oréal Factory
Aulnay-la-Barbière, France, 1992, Kathryn Gustafson

Set in the Parisian suburbs, the L'Oréal factory (by architects Valode and Pistre) expresses the giant cosmetic company's core values of precision, science and beauty. Described in the project outline as 'an unopened flower that encloses a secret garden at its heart', the site is essentially built form wrapped around an open interior of sensuously sculpted land and water. Landscape architect Kathryn Gustafson based her design of the 1.5-acre (0.6 hectares) site on ideas of the human body and refinement. A banked canal cuts through undulating earth; cross-sectional views of the earthwork are revealed by a linear footbridge that bisects the inner space. Plant textures become successively more refined toward the centre, where clipped grass lawns and a reflective pool mark the building's reception area. The flowing land- and water-form displays Gustafson's signature style of site topography as site-encompassing sculpture.

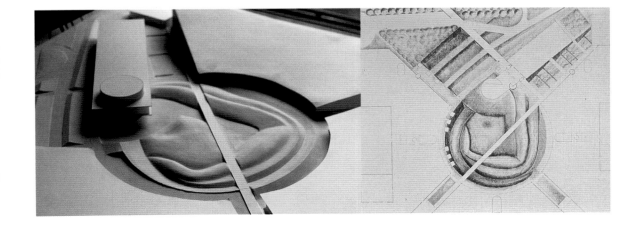

ATTENDING TO THE ORDINARY
Sweet Farm
Eastern Townships, Quebec, Canada,
1994–, PLANT/Lisa Rapoport, Christopher
Pommer, Mary Tremain. Landscape contractor:
Terrains Decoratifs

Lisa Rapoport says that gardens typically have
a 'tended intensity', an intricacy, an intimacy,
a concentration of elements that define their
existence. At Sweet Farm, Rapoport and partner
Christopher Pommer (both founding members
of PLANT) interceded in an 85-acre (34 hectares)
rural estate to bring forth a forest landscape
that is intrinsically subtle. After studying at length
the site's meadows, cliffs, gorges and tracts
of trees, the team put in place an open-ended
management plan. The strategy, based on the
idea of how rare it is that we actually take in and
consider the typical aspects of our environment,
brings idiosyncrasies and experiential moments
to the fore. In this sylvan setting, there are
no metaphors. Each object and event is just
what it is.

The clients' programme was simple – 'help
us use it more' – but the potential content was
more complex, involving mixed topographical
conditions and a variety of domestic, industrial
and agricultural remnants. In the course of their
very personal survey of the land, Rapoport and
Pommer first identified existing objects and areas
of interest and then drew a network of pathways,
some of which follow deer runs, others of which
lead through typical site conditions. The routes
are not about connecting exceptional places,
but about passing through – and truly engaging →

→ with – normal places. 'Interactions are imbued with movement, because it's about being in and moving through a very specific landscape,' explain the designers.

Fragments of site memory are actively incorporated, but are freed from past associations. Rusting mink cages become an open-air, leaf-strewn, moss-floored room; an abandoned car becomes an objet d'art; a mosaic of detritus caught in a dying pool is photographed and takes on meaning as displaced site text. By focusing the visitor's attention on unremarkable details (as opposed to the best views), Rapoport and Pommer set up a sensory reconnaissance – a process of exploration, which in today's landscape of signs, labels and aggressive programming is usually dormant.

In one spot, a cliff-top path opens onto a wood belvedere that projects into the tree canopy. Gaps between the boards reveal airspace below as the slope abruptly drops away. By provoking a sensation of vertigo, the construction forces one from the role of observer to participant. It is not about the objects themselves, but about creating vehicles of perception.

In another area, a path and small dock put the visitor in direct contact with creek water. The forest floor and flowing water are linked by a dock, and seasonal run-off is measured by water levels against the dock. Elsewhere within the forest grid, the touch of skis on snow creates a visual axis. In a sense, by objectifying certain transitory aspects of Sweet Farm, Rapoport and Pommer facilitate the highly subjective process of human interpretation.

They acknowledge that another designer, another client, would respond to the same site in a completely different way. But overall, they say, 'We need to engage people in the perception of the landscape in order to create future stewards of the land. By directing the ways in which people perceive the place – see, smell, and hear – [the landscape] is brought into focus.'

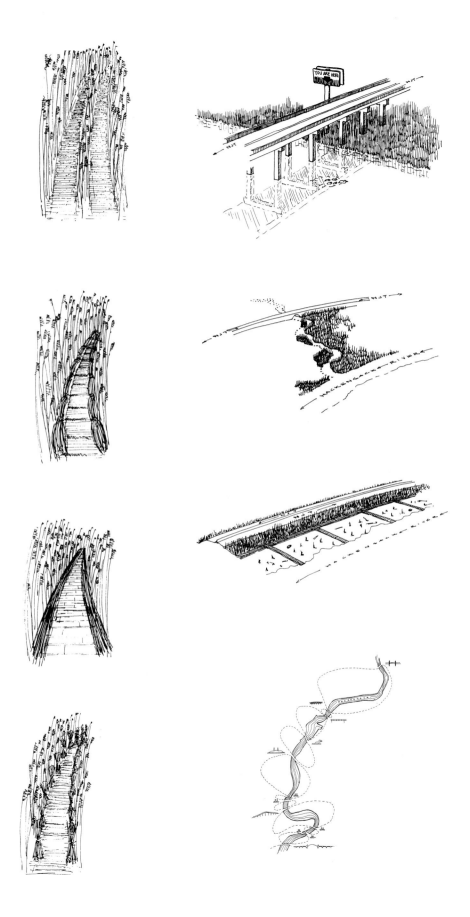

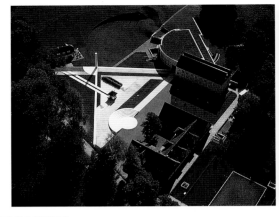

[left] **VALUE REASSIGNED**
Meadowlands Park
New Jersey, US, 2000, PLANT/Lisa Rapoport, Christopher Pommer,
Mary Tremain

Suggesting a prototype for the re-use of post-industrial sites (the most rapidly growing segment of landscape architecture), the Meadowlands Park scheme embodies a process of evaluation as opposed to prescribing a masterplan solution. Partners Rapoport, Pommer and Tremain spent days surveying the massive 20,000-acre (8940 hectares) parcel on the fringe of New York City, determining that interstitial spaces, discarded objects and undervalued physical conditions are potent artifacts of a site's past and future meaning. Their proposal is about re-viewing a landscape to reveal a complex conglomeration of overlapping stories. The team 'looked for patterns in the intimate details, as well as the overall picture', identifying the very unique parts that make up the whole. By deconstructing what is already there before adding new features, the optimal version – and, ideally, a new level of civic value – will emerge over time.

The sketches here are just a few of the many studies for the rediscovery of Meadowlands. Focusing on the creation of meaningful dialogue between existing visual and spatial characteristics of the land (many of which are culturally 'invisible') and outlying context, location- and geologically specific constructs help visitors to understand site conditions. In one area, a boardwalk threads through a previously inaccessible, grass-clogged wetland filled with junk and mystery. In another, humps and depressions in the terrain are signified with measuring and observation devices. Elsewhere, an exact visual axis between a narrow drainage channel and the World Trade Towers in Manhattan becomes a special viewing spot. The designers seek to re-establish Meadowlands in terms of public attitude and connection to a functional regional identity. At the same time, other groups are working on ecological restoration and wildlife issues. Simply put, PLANT's intention is to provide all parties with a different way of looking at and evaluating the infamous urban wetland. The 'sometimes jarring juxtaposition of nature with the flotsam of human existence' addresses changing notions of economic, aesthetic and public valuation.

[top and right] **A DIALOGUE OF OLD AND NEW**
Dorfplatz
Communication Center of Crédit Suisse, Zurich, Switzerland, 1995,
Dani Karavan

Sunlight, water, grass and an agricultural plantation work in concert with glass, blue neon and concrete to form a striking corporate composition. Located in a square between the historic residential area of Horgen and a modern communications centre, the Dorfplatz establishes a shared zone, belonging to neither neighbour but providing a platform for both. Primal civic gestures – a sundial and an amphitheatre – are connected by a concrete channel, down the centre of which runs a thin strand of blue neon. Inside a small existing house in the square, artist Dani Karavan planted an olive tree and inscribed a passage from the Book of Genesis on one wall. As described in the project literature, 'A dialog is being carried out between modern facilities and vernacular structures .... Karavan is not forcing the citizens to chose one or the other. He silently encourages them to accept the differences and make them work in their lives.'

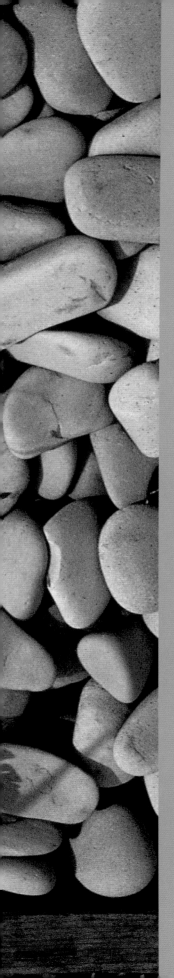

A NEW CHAPTER BEGINS
Thoreau Center for Sustainability
San Francisco, US, 1998, The Office of Cheryl Barton

In transforming a portion of the Presidio (a former military base) into a non-profit office complex, landscape architect Cheryl Barton saw an opportunity to establish a green standard for future development within the Presidio. Interested in sustainable site/building design and in cultural landscape rehabilitation, Barton decided that programmatic duality was a good thing. Thus, the design incorporates a water-harvesting system alongside subtle interpretations of site history. There is 'a play between phenomenology and context' on which the designer focuses our experience.

New design elements, such as hedges and walls recall the scale and layout of demolished buildings. Sections of old runnels, walkways and curbs contrast in colour, texture and character with newer materials. Aspects of sustainable design include increased permeability of paving surfaces,

replacement of grass with drought-tolerant species, removal of shade-heavy evergreens and installation of open-canopied flowering trees on the south side of the building. Water is collected and conducted through the site by new runnels that tie into the pre-existing system and will eventually feed a nearby wetland. Occasionally, Iris douglasiana [left], an indicator species for moisture, rise above water-rounded stones. Edging materials [overleaf] collect and conduct water in the 'runnel courts', and a detail of remnant curb marks a moment in time. The Thoreau Center deals, on different but complementary levels, with the idea of conserving precious resources. Be it water or cultural history, the landscape reveals an evolving narrative based on Henry David Thoreau's concept of our human relationship with nature.

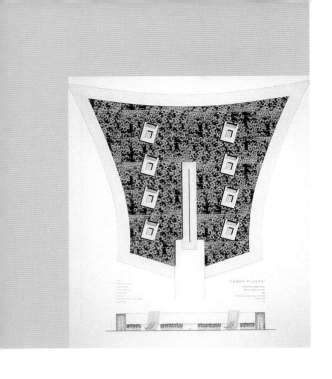

To relay information, designers incorporate natural elements of the site context into their built landscapes.

BASKING IN THE SUN
Power Plants
Festival International des Jardins, Chaumont-sur-Loire,
France, 1993, Peter Walker, William Johnson and
Partners

At the annual festival of contemporary gardens in the
Loire Valley, a limited palette of paving and planting
materials 'reduced the process of solar energy and
photosynthesis into an icon'.

Six striped lawn chairs and accompanying solar
panels set on green gravel pads, bask in a plot of
sunflowers. Nodding to the interdependence of man's
productivity and energy resources, Power Plants explores
various manifestations of the nature/technology dialectic
under the guise of sunbathing, the cultivation of an
agricultural crop and the collection and dispersal of solar
energy. Electricity generated by the solar panels powers
a fluorescent tube at the garden's centre, casting a green
glow on the plants.

For forward-looking place-makers of today,
the value of a site's story is more important
than formal and compositional concerns.

INHABITING SPECTRAL VISIONS
Mimmamakin (From the Depth)
Gelsenkirchen, Germany, 1997, Dani Karavan

Karavan seeks the spirit of peace by synchronizing memory of the past with a reductive, sometimes geometrically calibrated, representation of the present. In two abandoned coal plants in the Ruhr region, metaphor and symbolism re-present the defunct industry that once killed natural systems but that now gives rise to an exploration of the local area's post-industrial landscapes. Remnant coal piles and machinery host a paradoxical tropical planting of palm, olive and orange trees; on one wall, photographs of miners stare into the functionally cleansed but aesthetically charged space. Water, sound, smoke, video and neon light play parts in the overall effect of the installation. A master of political sculpture, Karavan's body of work was described by collector Giuliano Gori (in 'Dani Karavan's Return', Dani Karavan, catalogue for exhibition at Fort Belvedere in Florence, 1999, pp. 39–43) as 'always placing man with his rights and duties – within the context of a radically new aesthetic – at the center of life'. In From the Depth, visual impact is achieved with a limited language.

TEACHING FOR THE FUTURE
Earth Centre
South Yorkshire, UK, 1999, Grant Associates
(masterplan and landscape architecture)

A collection of content-rich gardens – living classrooms, really – are featured at the Earth Centre: Water-Conservation Gardens, Twenty-First-Century Gardens, Regeneration Gardens and Forest Gardens are found alongside Working Wetlands, Adventure Mound, Waterworks and Big Top. Part amusement ground, part museum, part public parkland, the vast (horti)cultural development on the banks of the River Don is built to impress on visitors the need to foster a sustainable environmental future. Integrated building, energy and production systems are plugged into the local ecosystems and urban and transportation networks in a mutually informative complex that offers 'green' versions of everyday activities. The Earth Centre and its hopeful exhibits provide a focus for the regeneration of the Don Valley and 420 acres

(170 hectares) of former coal fields. According to Grant Associates, 'it is designed to make people look, think and react to the issues that affect the future management of our landscape, our natural heritage'. Contemporary environmental concerns are approached through the merging of traditional land-management practices and innovative techniques.

A key aspect of the plan is the creation of a striking visual image, avoiding naturalistic scenes. To this end, wild flowers, grasses, cereals and other crops are graphically arranged. Belts and strategic blocks of woodland will eventually transform the site. Various zones reflect topographical and hydrological conditions. Almost all by-products are reused – water is collected, stored, cleansed on site – and specific gardens are intended to challenge prevailing notions of 'good' versus 'bad' horticultural practices and aesthetic expressions. Entrance is free, if you arrive by bicycle.

Books

Adams, William Howard and Stuart Wrede, eds. Denatured Visions: Landscape and Culture in the Twentieth Century (New York: The Museum of Modern Art, 1991).

Bachelard, Gaston. The Poetics of Space (New York: Orion Press, 1964).

Beardsley, John. Earthworks and Beyond: Contemporary Art in the Landscape (3rd ed. New York and London: Abbeville Press, 1998).

Berrizbeitia, Anita and Linda Pollak. Inside Outside: Between Architecture and Landscape (Gloucester, MA: Rockport, 1999).

Brown, Jane. The Modern Garden (London: Thames & Hudson, 2000).

Cooper, Guy and Gordon Taylor. Paradise Transformed: The Private Garden for the Twenty-First Century (New York: The Monacelli Press, 1996).

Corner, James, essays, drawings and commentary. Photographs Alex S. MacLean. Taking Measures Across the American Landscape (New Haven and London: Yale University Press, 1996).

Cora, Bruno, ed. Dani Karavan. Catalogue for exhibition at Fort Belvedere in Florence (Italy: gli ori: maschietto & musolino, 1999).

Cosgrove, Denis E. Social Formation and Symbolic Landscape (London: Croom Helm, 1984).

Eckbo, Garrett. Landscape for Living (New York, 1950).

Francis, Mark and Randolf T. Hester Jr., eds. The Meaning of Gardens: Idea, Place, and Action (Cambridge, MA: MIT Press, 1990).

Gillette, Jane, ed. Preserving Modern Landscape Architecture: Conference at Wave Hill (Berkeley, CA: Spacemaker Press, 1999).

Hall, Edward T. The Hidden Dimension (New York: Doubleday Anchor, 1966).

Imbert, Dorothée. The Modernist Garden in France (New Haven and London: Yale University Press, 1993).

Jewell, Linda, ed. Peter Walker: Experiments in Gesture, Seriality and Flatness (New York: Rizzoli, 1990).

Johnson, Jory, text. Photographs Felice Frankel. Modern Landscape Architecture: Redefining the Garden (New York: Abbeville Press, 1991).

Kassler, Elizabeth. Modern Gardens and the Landscape (New York: The Museum of Modern Art, 1964).

Kastner, Jeffrey and Brian Wallis. Land and Environmental Art (London: Phaidon Press, 1998).

Keeney, Gavin, John Dixon Hunt and Allen S. Weiss. On the Nature of Things (Boston, MA: Birkhäuser, 2001).

Kienast, Dieter. Kienast-Gardens (Basel: Birkhäuser, 1997).

Kurokawa, Kisho. Introduction by Dennis Sharp. Kuala Lumpur International Airport (Stuttgart: Edition Axel Menges, 1999).

Lefaivre, Liane and Alexander Tzonis. Architecture in Europe Since 1968: Memory and Invention (London: Thames & Hudson and New York: Rizzoli, 1992).

Lyall, Sutherland. Foreword by Geoffrey Jellicoe. Designing the New Landscape (London: Thames & Hudson, 1991).

McHarg, Ian. Design With Nature (Garden City, NY: Natural History Press, 1969).

Meinig, D.W., ed. The Interpretation of Ordinary Landscapes (New York: Oxford University Press, 1979).

Mosser, Monique and Georges Teyssot, eds. The History of Garden Design: The Western Tradition from the Renaissance to the Present Day (London: Thames & Hudson, 1991).

Müller, Hans-Jürgen and Helga. Mariposa (Lindinger + Schmid Kuntsprojekte und Verlag, 2001).

Spirn, Anne Whiston. The Granite Garden: Urban Nature and Human Design (New York: Basic Books, 1984).

Treib, Marc, ed. Modern Landscape Architecture: A Critical Review (Cambridge, MA: MIT Press, 1993).

Tunnard, Christopher. Gardens in the Modern Landscape (London: The Architectural Press, 1938).

Turner, B.L., ed. The Earth as Transformed by Human Action (Cambridge, MA: Cambridge University Press, 1990).

van Valkenburgh, Michael. Built Landscapes: Gardens in the Northeast (Brattleboro: Brattleboro Museum and Art Center, 1984).

Walker, Peter and Melanie Simo. Invisible Gardens: The Search for Modernism in the American Landscape (Cambridge, MA and London: MIT Press, 1994).

Weilacher, Udo. Forewords by John Dixon Hunt and Stephen Bann. Between Landscape Architecture and Land Art (Basel and Boston: Birkhäuser, 1996).

Nolan, Billy, ed. Essays by Henk van Blerck and Jörg Dettmar. 9+1 Young Dutch Landscape Architects (Rotterdam: NAi Publishers, 1999).

Articles/Features

Adams, William Howard. 'Breaking New Ground: Twentieth Century American Gardens'. Keeping Eden: A History of Gardening in America (Boston, MA and London: Little, Brown, and Company 1992).

Anderton, Frances. 'Avant-gardens'. Architectural Review (September 1989): 32–41.

Artes de Mexico. Selected interviews with Octavio Paz.

Bennett, Alan. 'Colour'. The Guardian Weekend (London, 11 December 1999): 35.

Barreneche, Raul. 'The Spirit of the New'. Architecture (April 2000).

Bottero, Maria. 'The Page in Berlin's Lindenstrasse, Kreuzberg'. Domus (October, 1998).

Brown, Brenda, ed. 'Eco-Revelatory Design: Nature Constructed/ Nature Revealed'. Landscape Journal (special issue, University of Wisconsin Press, 1998).

Chmiel, Peter. 'Calling Planet Earth'. Landscape Design (no. 281, June 1999).

'Dani Karavan'. Domus (October, 1998).

Dault, Gary Michael. 'The Garden as Art'. The Globe and Mail (July 2000).

den Ruijter, Michael. 'The Netherlands: Processes Versus Static States'. Topos (vol. 27, 1999).

Denecke, Dietrich. 'Ideology in the Planned Order Upon the Land'. Historical Geography (vol. 20:1, 1990).

Frampton, Kenneth. 'In Search of the Modern Landscape'. Denatured Visions: Landscape and Culture in the Twentieth Century (New York: The Museum of Modern Art, 1991).

Giovanni, Joseph. 'Through Los Angeles Starkly, Tarantino Style'. The New York Times (28 December 1997).

Hiss, Tony. 'Increasing the Volume'. Gardens Illustrated (February, 1999).

Howett, Catherine. 'Ecological Values in Twentieth-Century Landscape Design: A History and Hermeneutics'. Landscape Journal (special issue, 1998).

Irazabal, Clara and Fernanda Sanchez. 'The Transformation of Barcelona'. Urban Ecology Journal (no. 1, 1999).

Latz, Peter. 'The Idea of Making Time Visible'. Topos (December, 2000).

Lipman, Alan. 'Skating and Sliding to Art Decay'. The Independent on Sunday (7 March 1999).

Marx, Leo. 'The American Ideology of Space'. Denatured Visions: Landscape and Culture in the Twentieth Century (New York: The Museum of Modern Art, 1991).

Maude, Jane. 'Atlantic Utopia'. Architectural Review (August 1999).

Mendes da Rocha, Paulo. 'Consolidating a Site'. Pages Paysages (vol. 8).

Merchant, Carolyn. 'Partnership with Nature'. Landscape Journal (special issue, Madison: University of Wisconsin Press, 1998).

Meyer, Elizabeth. 'The Public Park as Avant-Garde (Landscape) Architecture'. Landscape Journal (Madison: University of Wisconsin Press).

Muschamp, Herbert. 'It's History Now, So Shouldn't Modernism Be Preserved, Too?' The New York Times (17 December 2000, section 2):1, 40.

Poole, Kathy. Civitas Oecologie: Infrastructure in the Ecological City'. Harvard Architectural Review (vol. 10, Princeton: Princeton Architectural Press, 1998).

———. 'Ecology as Content: A Subversive (Alternative) Approach to Ecological Design'. Paper presented at the annual meeting of the American Society of Landscape Architects, 1994.

Provoost, Michelle. 'O.M.A. at Almere: Becoming Commercial'. Topos (vol. 31, 2000).

Rafelman, Rachael. 'Hotbed of Ideas'. The Weekend Post (July 22, 2000).

Rattray, Fiona. 'Underground Force'. The Independent on Sunday (July 2000): 22–23.

Redhead, David. 'The Stuff That Surrounds Us'. The Guardian ('Space' section, 2 December 1999).

Rodriguez, Alicia. 'Celestial Connections'. Landscape Architecture (April, 1998).

———. 'Stone's Flow'. Landscape Architecture (August, 1997).

Spindler, Amy M. 'Radical Chic'. The New York Times ('Styles' section, 7 July 1999).

Syz, Francesca. 'Patterns in the Morning Dew'. New Eden (July/August 1999).

Thayer, Robert L. 'Pragmatism in Paradise'. Landscape (no. 3, vol. 30, 1990).

Weschler, Lawrence. 'When Fountainheads Collide'. The New Yorker (8 December 1997).

Magazines

Domus (Milan: Editoriale Domus).

Garten + Landschaft (Munich: Callwey Verlag).

Land Forum (Berkeley, CA: Spacemaker Press).

Landscape Architecture Magazine (Washington: American Society of Landscape Architects).

New Eden (London: IPC Magazines).

Pages Paysages (Versailles: Association Paysage et Diffusion).

Topos (Munich: Callwey Verlag).